Photo by Peter Cunningham

A scene from the New York production of "The Wake of Jamey Foster." Set designed by Santo Loquasto.

THE WAKE OF JAMEY FOSTER

BY
BETH HENLEY

DRAMATISTS
PLAY SERVICE
INC.

SPECIAL NOTE

Anyone receiving permission to produce THE WAKE OF JAMEY FOSTER is required (1) to give credit to the Author as sole and exclusive Author of the Play in all programs distributed in connection with performances of the Play and in all instances in which the title of the Play appears for purposes of advertising, publicizing or otherwise exploiting the Play and/or a production thereof; the name of the Author must appear on a separate line, in which no other name appears, immediately beneath the title and in size of type equal to 50% of the largest letter used for the title of the Play. No person, firm or entity may receive credit larger or more prominent than that accorded the Author and (2) to give the following acknowledgments on the title page of all programs distributed in connection with performances of the Play:

World Premiere at Hartford Stage Company, Hartford, Connecticut

SOUND EFFECTS

The following is a list of sound effects referenced in this Play:

Dog barking
Telephone ring
Auto sounds

World Premiere at Hartford Stage Company, Hartford, Connecticut.

THE WAKE OF JAMEY FOSTER was presented on Broadway by FDM Productions, Francois De Menil/Harris Maslansky, Elliot Martin, Ulu Grosbard, Nan Pearlman and Warner Theatre Productions Inc. at the Eugene O'Neill Theatre, in New York City, on October 14, 1982. It was directed by Ulu Grosbard; the setting was by Santo Loquasto; costumes were by Jennifer von Mayrhauser; lighting was by Jennifer Tipton; sound was by David Rapkin; and the associate producer was Arla Manson. The cast, in order of appearance, was as follows:

MARSHAEL FOSTER ....Susan Kingsley
LEON DARNELL ....Stephen Tobolowsky
KATTY FOSTER ....Belita Moreno
WAYNE FOSTER ....Anthony Heald
COLLARD DARNELL ....Patricia Richardson
PIXROSE WILSON ....Holly Hunter
BROCKER SLADE ....Brad Sullivan

SYNOPSIS OF SCENES

The action of the play takes place throughout Marshael Foster's house and yard in Canton, Mississippi.

ACT I

Scene 1: Morning
Scene 2: Supper Time

ACT II

Scene 1: Late that night
Scene 2: Throughout the night
Scene 3: The following morning

"FOR MAYPOE AND CHARLIE"

THE CAST

MARSHAEL FOSTER, 33, Jamey's widow
LEON DARNELL, 25, Marshael's brother
KATTY FOSTER, 29, Wayne's wife
WAYNE FOSTER, 29, Jamey's brother; Katty's husband
COLLARD DARNELL, 30, Marshael's sister
PIXROSE WILSON, 17, Leon's friend; an orphan
BROCKER SLADE, 53, Marshael's friend

THE SETTING

The entire action of the play takes place at Marshael Foster's house. The rooms that are visible are: the parlor; the front hall with stairs leading to the upstairs hall; Marshael's bedroom; and an outside area along the right side of the house. The house is an old rambling country home that is in distinct disrepair with faded drapes, peeling paint, old furniture, worn out rugs, etc. Throughtout the house books, papers, journals, etc. are scattered about, as evidence of Jamey's excessive though incomplete historical research. In the front hall there is a grandfather clock, a love seat, and a card table with chair that has been temporarily set out for the occasion. There is a front door Up Center. There is also a door that leads to the parlor. The furniture in the parlor has been rearranged to leave a vacant space for the expected

4

coffin. Several funeral wreaths and flower arrangements surround this area. The second door in the front hall, which is Stage Left, is a dining room door that leads to the rest of the downstairs. Upstairs the hallway has one exit leading to Marshael's bedroom. The bedroom is by far the most cluttered room in the house. There is a bed, a vanity with stool, a chaise lounge, a table with a world globe, a sewing machine, a dress dummy, a clothes rack with pink and gold drill team outfits on it in different stages of completion, and several boxes of household improvement items that are stacked against the wall. There is also a closet, a door leading to the bathroom, an Upstage window, and a balcony Stage Right. The Upstage window looks out onto the front yard. The balcony looks over the side yard. In the outside area there is a tree that grows at least as high as the balcony.

THE TIME

Spring

THE WAKE OF
JAMEY FOSTER

ACT I

Scene 1

*The lights go up on stage. It is morning. Upstairs,
Marshael Foster, 33, is sitting on her bed. She is
thin with shoulder length, curly hair and deep set
haunted eyes. She wears a black dress. Marshael pulls
a chocolate Easter rabbit out of an Easter basket and
bites off the top of its ears. She has another bite,
then rises, picks up a ladies' magazine and drops
back down onto her bed. She lies glancing through
the magazine; gnawing on the ears of the chocolate
rabbit.*

KATTY'S VOICE. (*Offstage.*) Go on and set them in there
with the other flowers. (*Leon Darnell, 25, enters the front
hall from the dining room. Leon is tall and gangly. He wears
a white shirt and a dark skinny tie with black Sunday pants
that are a bit high-waisted. He carries two large flower arrangements that he is swinging haphazardly about.*)
LEON. Where?! (*Katty Foster, 29, follows him into the
room carrying a small arrangement of flowers in a basket.*

7

Katty is pretty in a baby-doll-matron sort of way. She is still wearing a beehive hairdo that was popular when she was in college.)

KATTY. I'll arrange them myself. You just set them down there. In the parlor.

LEON. (*As he moves into the parlor.*) All right! Fine. 'Cause my angel is arriving today!

KATTY. (*Setting her basket down.*) These'll look real nice right out here on the card table by the memorial book—don't you think?

LEON. (*Swinging the baskets of flowers around the parlor.*) 'Cause she's riding in to see me.

KATTY. Do you think that we should serve the mourners any refreshments?

LEON. Riding in on the Greyhound express!

KATTY. Do you suppose just assorted beverages will do? I don't know what's called for—I've never done all this before—Oh no, Leon; not there! We have to leave some room. (*She moves the flowers away from the area reserved for the coffin.*)

LEON. Well, look, I'm going. I gotta get those soda bottles cashed in—got a car load.

KATTY. Oh, wait, Leon! Has anyone heard further from your sister, Collard?

LEON. Due in yesterday; that's the latest. Ah! (*He steps on a large tack and sits down to pull it out of his shoe.*)

KATTY. (*Arranging the flowers.*) Oh, mercy, I hope she's all right. Heavens knows, she should be used to driving up and down the highways of this state. But life is so full of unknown horror—

LEON. (*Pulling out a tack with a pocket knife.*) Collard's coming, she said she's coming—She always comes home when anybody dies. Wow! Look at the size of that tack!

KATTY. Why, here, let me throw that thing away! Where'd it come from, anyway?

LEON. (*Pondering his shoe.*) It's Pixrose I'm anxious on.

KATTY. Why, she's not due in till twelve noon? (*About*

the tack.) Maybe it dropped out of one of these folding chairs.

LEON. It's just—It's just I love her so much! I do. I love her. Oh, and she loves me too. She does. Is my hair looking funny down in front where Margarite Roper yanked out that handful?

KATTY. It could stand a comb.

LEON. (*Pulling out his comb.*) See, we're exactly alike. Pixrose and me. We're exactly the same. Both of us enjoy public transportation and both of us have bumps right here on our heads. (*Showing her.*) Look! We do! We do!

WAYNE'S VOICE. (*Offstage.*) Katty! Katty! Katherine! (*Wayne Foster appears on the upstairs landing, as Katty and Leon move into the front hall. Wayne, 29, is an attractive man with cold, nervous eyes.*)

KATTY. (*Overlapping.*) What?! Yes, darling! What?!

WAYNE. (*Running on.*) My cuff links—the silver ones with the monograms. Did you forget to pack them?

KATTY. Why, I hope not. Did you check your little jewel case.

WAYNE. I've checked everything—all the luggage! Look, here, my cuff are totally undone!

KATTY. Well, now, I'll go take a look myself.

WAYNE. And nobody's doing a thing about Marshael's children. She's supposed to be getting them dressed! One's got gum all stuck in it's ears and hair—

KATTY. Oh, dear, Leon, quick, you bring me those scissors from in there. (*Leon goes to get scissors from the parlor. As she straightens his collar.*) Now just hush down, Honey Lamb. Why we're all gonna do every little bitty thing we can do to unburden poor, old Papa Sweet Potato.

LEON. (*Slinging the scissors.*) Here, catch!

WAYNE. My God!

KATTY. (*Overlapping.*) Leon!

WAYNE. And just what is he doing inviting strange house quests over, as if we don't have misery enough to deal with?!

KATTY. She's not a house guest, Angel Cake, she's a homeless refugee.

LEON. She's my girl!

WAYNE. I don't care what she is. I need my time of grief. I need my solitude. God.

KATTY. I know. Of couse, you do. It's awful. But try to be charitable, darling. Two entire wings of that orphanage were destroyed, and it seems Leon is the only obliging friend that child has.

WAYNE. Friend?! Ha! He hardly knows her.

LEON. Hardly know her?! Ha! Why, I've kissed her!

KATTY. Oh, please, now, honey, go on and force yourself to eat some breakfast. It'll do you good. I'll go up and check on those children and find your cuff links for you. (*On her way upstairs.*) I know I packed them. They gotta be there. (*She exits down the upstairs hall.*)

LEON. (*Turning back to face Wayne.*) And guess what? We both hate Dr. Peppers and Orange Crushes are our favorite beverage. Both of us.

WAYNE. Forget it, Leon. I'm sorry. I'm on the edge here. You understand. It's been a blow.

LEON. Yeah. I'm lucky. I never had a brother. Well, gotta go cash in them bottles.

WAYNE. Leon, would you wait here a minute?

LEON. What is it?

WAYNE. I just wanted to know what all went on with Marshael yesterday afternoon over at the funeral parlor? I mean what all did she decide on?

LEON. Well, not much. 'Cept she said for me to handle it, and so I did. I handled it all.

WAYNE. You mean, she left the arrangements entirely in your hands? She let you settle on everything—all by yourself?

LEON—Yeah. 'Cept for the coffin. She pointed at it and said, "That's the one." Then she tells me she needs to get home and dye up some Easter eggs; so I'm supposed to handle it all. And I did too. Precisely that.

WAYNE. Well, I certainly would have hoped that the

details and arrangements of my only brother's funeral would have concerned his wife more than coloring up a batch of goddamn Easter eggs! (*Upstairs, Marshael puts down the bunny, leaves the bedroom and exits up the hall.*)

LEON. Now look here, Willie Wayne, I handled it all. Picked out a nice cheerful suit for Jamey to be wearing here today. Took down a dress shirt and matching tie. Why, I even signed him up for a shave, shampooing and manicure. He's gonna look his best.

WAYNE. It's just I—I want it done proper. He's my brother. I want things done with class and dignity and respect.

LEON. Well, I'm the one you want in charge then. See, I ordered this memorial book here and a solid blanket of roses for the coffin. Why, tommorrow we've got us a limousine being escorted by a policeman on a motorcycle. I even got us black arm bands to pass out and black veils for the ladies I got the works! No need to worry, Willie Wayne. No need at all.

COLLARD'S VOICE. (*Offstage*) Hello! Wooh! Hey, I made it! I'm home! How's Mashy?! (*The front door flies open and Collard Darnell enters in a muddy red evening gown and a pair of men's cowboy boots that are several sizes too large. She carries a large straw bag. Her hair is wild and her face is dirty. She is thirty years old.*)

LEON. (*Overlapping.*) Collard! You?! Collard Greens! Collard Greens!!

COLLARD. (*Overlapping as she hugs him.*) Leon! Baby boy! Baby boy!

LEON. I told you she'd make it! I told ya!

COLLARD. (*Stopping.*) Well, hi ya, Willie Wayne! Let's see, car exploded; suitcase stolen; and shoes stuck in the Memphis mud. It's funny, Willie Wayne, but I always know just what you're gonna say even before you open your mouth.

WAYNE. I wasn't gonna say anything, Collard. Nothing you do surprises me much less your lack of concern for your bereaved sister. Excuse me, but I've got to go see if I can

11

force some breakfast down this lump in my throat. (*He exits out the dining room door.*)

COLLARD. How do people get like that? How the hell do they do it?

LEON. Must be born to it.

COLLARD. I suppose he's not even gonna acknowledge the Get Well Soon card I sent t'Jamey. Pompous little pig. Shit. Well, home again, home again, jigady jig. (*Pause.*) So Jamey's really dead?

LEON. Looks like it.

COLLARD. How's Marshy taking it?

LEON. Seems t'be doing all right.

COLLARD. Well, shit. So how'd it happen? Willie Wayne's giving me this song and dance about some sorta head injury. Didn't sound all that serious when I got the call last Sunday.

LEON. Well, I guess it was pretty serious cause by Wednesday noon he's dead.

COLLARD. Jesus.

LEON. Seems that head injury he'd acquired caused him to have a stroke Tuesday evening, paralyzing one half of his entire body. Then Wednesday 'bout noon time . . .

COLLARD. (*Finding her cigarettes.*) Lord. So how'd he get this head injury? He run into some wood post?

LEON. No, he's kicked in the head by a cow.

COLLARD. He's what?!

LEON. Right out in the field over by Cambden on Highway 17. I suppose he'd had quite a load t'drink.

COLLARD. Out boozing in a field and gets kicked in the head by a cow. What the hell was he doing out there?

LEON. Chasing cows, I guess.

COLLARD. Holy Church of the Lord. You got a light?

LEON. (*Moving into the parlor.*) In here. There are matches galore right here in this dish—

COLLARD. (*Entering the parlor.*) What's all this? What's happening here? What's all the crap? Jesus!

LEON. They're setting up for the exhibition of the body—for the wake.

COLLARD. A wake? Here? In this house? Aren't they going to use a funeral home like most decent, civilized folks?

LEON. Jamey's mother wanted it here. She says that's how it's been done for generations in her family up in north Mississippi 'round Tubler.

COLLARD. God. Poor Marshy. She must be going to pieces 'bout now.

LEON. Well, I'm seeing that she's gonna have some close personal relatives and friends t'help t'get her through this long and desolate night.

COLLARD. (Looking around slowly at the flowers.) Close relatives? Swell, like Willie Wayne and his bee-hive wife.

LEON. Well, yeah, there's them and there's you and also I've called in Mr. Brocker Slade.

COLLARD. Who's he?

LEON. Close personal friend of Marshael's. He built her them new red kitchen chairs. You'll like him for sure. He's done it all. Everything. He's eaten certified dog meat in China and he's got tattoos up and down his arms and legs both.

COLLARD. (Still dazed by all the flowers.) Sounds remarkable t'me.

LEON. Oh, he's absolutely your style of person. I told him to please come over and help stand guard over the body here tonight. Just by chance peculiar things start t'happening.

COLLARD. (With a shudder.) Well, I'll just bet our Mama and Daddy are rolling over in their sweet graves right about now at the thought of those North Mississippi dirt farmers bringing a rotting old carcass right into our very home.

LEON. Well, it ain't our home anymore.

COLLARD. No, not since Jamey Foster took it over lock, stock, and barrel with his dusty books and pamphlets and idiotic papers. Imagine, we used to play dominoes right down here on this torn up rug.

LEON. You and me live other places now.

COLLARD. Oh, I know it. It's these bright flowers here giving me the jumping jitters. They make the whole place look morbid and scary. Now look here, I'm practically on the verge of tears.

LEON. Why, Collard. Collard Greens, what's wrong? I'll save ya.

COLLARD. (*Crying.*) Oh, it's nothing. Just I—I really could have been here earlier to help Marshy out with things —I told her I'd be here, but it's my Easter vacation, you know, and I didn't want t'spend the time watching some man die in a hospital. Shit. I already tried doing that with Daddy.

LEON. Well, nobody was for sure he'd die. Nobody guessed it.

COLLARD. (*Wiping her eyes with her red skirt.*) But even after I knew he was already dead, I went on up t'Memphis for a wild party. That's why I didn't make it home yesterday. I'm a shit. A hopeless shit! Oh, but you should see the car G.W. Porter lent me t'get down here in—a beautiful, white, Cadillac convertible.

LEON. No kidding?

COLLARD. Go on and take a look at it. It's parked out there in the street. See it?

LEON. Wow!! A cloud! Why, it looks just like a big, fat white cloud! Can I—Could I go out—

COLLARD. No, you can't! Don't even touch it! I can't afford t'get it all smudged up.

LEON. But I could sit in it, couldn't I? Just sit in it. I mean, when my girl comes—My girl! Oh, brother, I gotta go get those bottles turned on in. (*Racing to the front hall.*)

COLLARD. What girl? What bottles? What're you talking? (*She follows him into the front hall.*)

LEON. My girl, Pixrose, she's arriving at twelve noon. I gotta get those empty bottles turned on in so I can afford t'get her a precious remembrance.

COLLARD. (*In the front hall.*) Jesus, are you back t'gathering up those goddam coke bottles?! What happened to your paper route?

LEON. Why, Collard Greens, you're not up to date. I have

14

me a permanent full time job now. Them bottles are strictly sideline. Well, I gotta run, Marshael wants me back before they arrive with—well, with the body. See ya!

COLLARD. Yeah. (*Leon exits slamming the door, Katty enters through the upstairs hallway. She carries the cufflinks.*)

KATTY. Wayne?! Baby, I found your silver—(*Spotting Collard as she comes down the stairs.*) Why, Collard! Honey, when did you arrive? We were so anxious for your safety—Why, my you're—all dressed in red.

COLLARD. It's the only stitch I got, Katty. Rest a my clothes was filched up in Memphis.

KATTY. Filched? How utterly astounding. How astounding. What were you doing up in Memphis?

COLLARD. (*Uncomfortable.*) Oh, on a visit.

KATTY. Well, I just don't know what you're gonna wear. The people will be arriving from ten this morning on. Do you think you could find something of Marshael's that might be suitable? You see, the only clothes I brought are strictly organized. I mean, I'm wearing this outfit all day today, and then tomorrow I'm wearing my navy blue suit with my navy pumps and my navy dress hat with the white piping.

COLLARD. Forget it Katty, I'll manage.

KATTY. But, of course now, if you feel you could fit into my navy outfit, I suppose you could wear it today. I mean, you're welcome to try it.

COLLARD. (*Going into the parlor.*) It's all right.

KATTY. (*Following her.*) I could wash and iron it out tonight so I could still wear it tomorrow morning for the funeral. That is if Marshael has all the cleaning apparatus that I'll be needing.

COLLARD. Look, Katty, I don't want to wear your navy suit. I don't like navy. It reminds me too much of blue.

KATTY. Well, pardon me, I'm sure. I was just trying to be gracious. (*Pause.*) We're all overwrought. (*Pause.*) Reverand Rigby says sudden violent deaths are the most difficult to deal with. (*Pause.*) So, how's your job going?

15

COLLARD. Swell, I'm on vacation from it.

KATTY. Oh, right. How stupid of me. How could you be taking school portraits of the children when they're all out for their Easter holidays.

COLLARD. It'd be hard.

KATTY. (*Laughing.*) Oh, it would be. I tell you. I've always envied your job. How you get to travel all over the state—going to all the public and parochial schools—taking pictures of those precious children—thinking up amusing tricks to make them smile—driving in a company car—seeing the world.

COLLARD. Right.

KATTY. Oh, by the by, Mother Foster asked me to see if I could implore you to take some memorial pictures for her of, well, of Jamey. Since you're the professional in the family, we thought you could do them really nicely.

COLLARD. Well, I didn't bring my photographic equipment home with me—

KATTY. Oh, that's alright. We've got a camera right here that's got a flash attachment for the indoors and everything. You could take the shots as soon as the body arrives—before we open up the room for all the mourners.

COLLARD. I'm sorry, Katty. I—I just don't like t'look at dead people. Look, I gotta go change. I'm tired. I gotta lie down.

KATTY. Oh, Collard, wait! Wayne and I are staying in your old room. (*Collard stops.*) We moved James Jr. in with his sisters. Course the children are all going over to your Aunt Muffin's for tonight. That way they won't have to be here with the wake and all going on. It might could frighten little children.

COLLARD. It might could.

KATTY. Anyway, this friend of Leon's coming in and she's gonna stay up in the children's room. That means you'll be sleeping with Marshael in her room for tonight. I'm sure she can use the company.

COLLARD. Fine.

16

KATTY. (*Trying to grab hold of Collard's straw bag.*) Here, let me help you with your bag? You look tired.

COLLARD. I got it.

KATTY. No, really—I'll get it—

COLLARD. Katty—(*A few things fall from the bag, among them a small pink sack.*)

KATTY. Oh, mercy, here—some things dropped out. Here you go. Just call me butter fingers.

COLLARD. (*About the sack.*) Oh, well, that's for you anyway, if you want it.

KATTY. For me? How thoughtful. (*She opens the sack.*) Why, look, it's a pair of spring booties with sweet, little yellow ribbons.

COLLARD. I saw 'em in a store window. I thought with the baby coming in the winter—maybe it'd be able to wear 'em by next spring.

KATTY. (*Shaken.*) Oh, well, thank you, Collard. But I lost the baby. It's not gonna be coming. I don't know what t'do with the present I—I guess I'll just give it back t'you.

COLLARD. Katty.

KATTY. I gotta go see to Marshael's kids. I gotta go get 'em ready. (*She exits down the upstairs hall.*)

COLLARD. Katty—(*Slinging the booties back in her bag.*) Jesus! (*She takes a deep breath and opens the door to Marshael's room.*) Marshy? (*She is intensely relieved to find no one is there. She takes a moment to notice the rack of marching costumes, sighs, then drops her bag down and sinks onto the bed. There is a knock at the front door. Collard pulls a boot off and slings it against the wall. A second knock is heard. Collard slings off her other boot. After a third knock Wayne enters from the dining room carrying a cloth napkin and a half eaten piece of toast.*)

WAYNE. What's wrong around here? Doesn't anyone have the good manners to open a door? Must I do it all? Everything?! (*He opens the door. Pixrose Wilson, 17, stands on the other side holding a small torn up suitcase. Pixrose wears red stockings and a long sleeved dress. She has sunken eyes, long, stringy hair and white, white skin.*) Hello. Oh. Won't you come in.

PIXROSE. Much obliged.

WAYNE. I'm Wayne Foster, the, ah, brother of the deceased.

PIXROSE. I'm Pixrose Wilson from the Sacred Heart Orphonage Asylum.

WAYNE. Yes, well, we're glad to have you, Prissrose.

PIXROSE. It's Pix. Like fix.

WAYNE. Oh, of course, Pix. Here, let me take your luggage for you.

PIXROSE. Thank you, sir. That's very obliging.

WAYNE. Well, why don't you come into the parlor and take a seat. (*They start into the parlor.*) I don't believe Leon was expecting you till about twelve noon.

PIXROSE. Well, I started early and got myself a ride on back of a milk truck. That way I was able to save my bus fare in it's entirety.

WAYNE. That's very economical of you. They do say "A penny saved is a penny earned."

PIXROSE. Is this where they're gonna be setting down the body?

WAYNE. Why, yes. I, ah, hope you don't find it too upsetting.

PIXROSE. What's that?

WAYNE. A, well, a body. The presence of a body in the house.

PIXROSE. (*With a silght, slight shrug.*) It won't be going nowhere.

WAYNE. Well, ah, it is regrettable, Pixrose, that your, ah, stay falls at what is a time of grave personal tragedy for our family. I do hope that you'll be able to bear with us through our grief. Won't you have a seat? (*Pause.*) Leon should be returning any minute. Probably very soon. He'll be back. Would you like some breakfast?

PIXROSE. No, sir.

WAYNE. How about some coffee?

PIXROSE. I appreciate it, sir, but I don't believe I'm feeling thirsty.

WAYNE. Hmm. Well, we were all very distressed to hear about the fire over at the orphanage. It appears the damage was quite extensive.

PIXROSE. Yes. It's a terrible crime—arson.

WAYNE. Arson? Was it actually arson?

PIXROSE. Oh, no doubt in my mind.

WAYNE. Arson. How loathesome, inflicting misery and terror on a group of helpless children.

PIXROSE. Well, fortunately, I was able to drop some of the small infants out from the windows and down into the azalea bushes below.

WAYNE. It must have been quite a terrifying episode for you.

PIXROSE. Why, it certainly was. Particularly as I've been afflicted by fire most of my entire life.

WAYNE. How do you mean?

PIXROSE. Well it started out my mama hating the house we lived in. She used t'say it was trashy. She'd sit around in the dark holding lit matches—always threatening to burn this trashy house down—and one day she did it. She lit up the dining room curtains, loosing flames over the entire house and charcoaling herself to death as a final result.

WAYNE. My God.

PIXROSE. It's a terrible crime, arson. Caused me t'get burns all over the lower parts of my body.

WAYNE. (*Rubbing his forehead.*) That's horrible.

PIXROSE. (*Pulling at her stockings.*) Well, I can cover up the scars by wearing these leg stockings.

WAYNE. I see.

PIXROSE. I just wish my arms hadn't caught on fire in that automobile explosion. I used t'like to look at 'em. But, of course, my daddy, he died an instantaneous death, and my brother, Franky suffered permanent brain damage; so I guess I was just lucky t'be flung burning from outta the car. That explosion was also diagnosed as deliberate arson.

WAYNE. I don't feel well. My nose——
PIXROSE. Arson . . . It's a terrible, terrible crime.
WAYNE. Excuse me. I'm bleeding. I apologize. (*About his nose.*) This damnable business. How disturbing. This is extreme. (*The phone begins ringing, as he runs out of the room bringing the napkin up to his massively bloody nose. Upstairs Collard throws a pillow over her head. As he exits out the dining room.*) I can't get it now—I can't do everything! My nose . . . it's—It's sickening. (*The phone stops ringing. Pixrose goes to look at the drops of blood that have fallen from Wayne's nose. Marshael appears on the upstairs landing. Pixrose gently presses the drops of blood into the carpet with the toe of her shoe then goes to sit down on the sofa. Marshael goes into her bedroom. Collard turns to see her.*)
MARSHAEL. Collard! Coll, you're home! You're here! You're home!
COLLARD. (*Overlapping as she jumps out of bed.*) Marshy! Marshy! Marsh! Are you doing all right? How are you doing?
MARSHAEL. (*Opening her mouth.*) Look—look, here— canker sores! All over my mouth! I'm in pain; I'm not kidding: I'm about to die! Do you see 'em? They're all purple and swollen
COLLARD. God. Well—Well, get yourself some salt water and start t'gargling. That looks awful!
MARSHAEL. Oh, hell, I've been gargling my mouth raw, but just to no avail. Well, so you're looking awfully fine. I see ya came dressed for the occasion.
COLLARD. (*Uncomfortable.*) Yeah, well, I gotta borrow something a somebody's. (*Getting up to get a cigarette.*) Hey. I'm sorry I'm late. I don't mean t'keep relentlessly letting everyone down. Some unavoidable circumstances.
MARSHAEL. Doesn't matter.
COLLARD. Now that I'm here I'll try to help out. What needs to be done?
MARSHAEL. Nothing.

COLLARD. I could order some flowers or call up a church or something.

MARSHAEL. It's all taken care of.

COLLARD. Well, I'll try not to screw things up. (*About the costumes on the clothes rack.*) God, what the hell's all this?

MARSHAEL. Oh, my costumes. I'm making the marching dresses for all of next year's Prancing' Ponies.

COLLARD. Jesus, they're still using those same awful colors. And look, they've still got the same tacky tassels and vests to go with 'em. Praise God, I always had sense enough to stay out of that fascist organization. How many of these ya gotta make?

MARSHAEL. Oh, this is only the beginning you see right here. I've got about twenty more t'cut out.

COLLARD. Well, you're mighty industrious.

MARSHAEL. You're telling me (*Kicking a sealed box.*) Look, here, I've even taken to selling household improvement ornaments.

COLLARD. What're they?

MARSHAEL. Oh, you know; things like wall light fixtures and decorative place mats—salt and pepper shakers shaped like crocodiles. A load of junk.

COLLARD. When'd you start doing all this?

MARSHAEL. Been at it a long while. Gotta keep busy. I, ah, can show you the catalogue if you want—(*She gets catalogue.*)

COLLARD. No, that's all right. I don't use place mats.

MARSHAEL. Oh . . . Sure.

COLLARD. (*Pause.*) So. Well. Gosh. I'm sorry.

MARSHAEL. Yeah. Well. Heck.

COLLARD. He was a real smart man. I know he would have been able to publish his work in time. He was just so awfully young.

MARSHAEL. You think? Nah. he's thirty-five. He'd put on plenty of weight and started losing his hair. He'd even de-

21

veloped this sorta rash all over his knuckles. He'd always get nervous and start t'rubbing it. He wasn't that young. Everyone's saying he died so young. He wasn't really. He'd changed alot.

COLLARD. Well, I didn't mean to imply he was a spring chicken or anything.

MARSHAEL. No. (*Pause.*) Oh, do you hear those birds chirping outside.

COLLARD. Yeah.

MARSHAEL. They're right out my window. They've made a nest down there on the ledge. Go on and look. (*Collard goes to the window.*) See it. I saw some eggs in their nest. They were speckled.

COLLARD. Oh . . . I see it. Yes. Your very own bird's nest. (*Katty comes down the hall and knocks at Marshael's door. She carries a blue satin ribbon.*)

KATTY. Marshael, honey?

MARSHAEL. Yes?

KATTY. (*Entering the bedroom.*) Hi. Listen, Mr. Mommett called from the funeral home. He said the hearst is on its way. They should be arriving any minute.

MARSHAEL. All right.

KATTY. I'll go downstairs to greet them.

MARSHAEL. That's good.

KATTY. Oh, one more thing. Do you mind me twisting Cherry Lee's braids up into a bun on top of her head? She said she likes the way it looks.

MARSHAEL. No, I appreciate it, Katty. It's real nice of you.

KATTY. Good. Then I'll go on and put the bow in it. Bye bye now. (*Katty exits. Collard starts to pull at her hair.*)

COLLARD. (*In a whisper.*) God. Rip out my soul.

MARSHAEL. What?

COLLARD. Tear out my heart with jagged glass.

MARSHAEL. What—

COLLARD. Oooh, I just gave Katty baby booties—for her new baby.

MARSHAEL. Oh, God, no one told you? She lost the baby about three weeks ago. It makes her third miscarriage.

COLLARD. It does?

MARSHAEL. She keeps going out to that fertility clinic, but it never seems to work out for her.

COLLARD. I could die.

MARSHAEL. Oh, it's not your fault. You didn't know. I should have called you.

COLLARD. But you know, the funny thing is, Marshy . . . I sensed it. For some reason I sensed she'd lost it. But I just gave her the booties anyway.

MARSHAEL. Why would you do that?

COLLARD. I don't know. I'm a black sheep. A black, black soul. (*A car is heard pulling up.*)

MARSHAEL. (*Rushing out onto the balcony.*) God, that's probably them. Oh, it is! I don't believe it! Look at that horrible black car. This whole thing's a joke! I could just about eat fire! So this is how he finally returns to the house. It's so humiliating. So cheap.

COLLARD.(*Overlapping.*)What are you saying? Marshy, what's wrong?

MARSHAEL. Oh, he'd abandoned me. Four months ago. Abandonment.

COLLARD. He did? But you never said. You never called me. I wish you'd call me.

MARSHAEL. Well, I just kept thinking if the blood ever dried he'd be back home. Foolish notion. I got over it. Filed for divorce not two weeks ago. Now he pulls this little stunt. Thinks he can leave it all in my lap to sort out and make right. Well, as you can see, I've got mixed emotions about the entire event.

COLLARD. I don't wonder you do. (*Leon enters from the dining room below.*)

LEON. Pixrose? Pixrose! I heard you'd arrived! They told me you'd arrived!

PIXROSE. I have, Leon! I'm here! Right here!

23

MARSHAEL. (*Hanging over the balcony railing.*) Look, there it comes—the box he's in. They're lifting it out of the car.

COLLARD. My God, they are!

LEON. (*Finding her in the parlor.*) Why, you've finally arrived.

PIXROSE. I know—I have. (*They stare at each other.*)

COLLARD. I hope they're careful. It looks awfully flimsy.

MARSHAEL. It oughta be. It was the cheapest pinebox they had. (*Lights fade to blackout. End of scene.*)

ACT I

Scene 2

It is evening. The door to the parlor is closed. Pixrose's suitcase has been removed. A cheap pine lift-lid coffin has been set up inside the room. The upper half of the lid has been removed from the case and left leaning against a nearby wall. Thus part of the corpse is visible. It wears a bright orange and yellow plaid jacket.

Marshael sits on the stairway in the front hall drinking a glass of gin and eating jelly beans that she carries in her dress pocket. After a moment, she throws a jellybean at the umbrella stand. It lands inside. She tries two more jellybeans that miss. She pauses a moment—looks at the closed parlor door and throws a jellybean at it. She goes back to drinking her gin.

Leon enters from the dining room L., carrying a plate and some silverware.

24

LEON. How ya doing?

MARSHAEL. Fine.

LEON. I brought out your food for you. You didn't touch nothing on your whole plate.

MARSHAEL. I'm not hungry.

LEON. I know, but ya need t'try and eat something. I swear, I haven't seen ya eat or sleep for three days now. Your eyes are blood red.

MARSHAEL. I feel fresh.

LEON. Just try some of your ham. It's awfully good. Annie Hart sent it over. Go on have a bite. Try it. You're gonna like it. (*A pause as he looks at her waiting for her to eat.*)

MARSHAEL. I can't eat with you watching over me. Go on back to the kitchen and finish your supper. Go on now, Leon. I'll eat it.

LEON. All right. (*He starts to leave, then stops.*) Hey, Marshael?

MARSHAEL. What?

LEON. Do you like Pixrose?

MARSHAEL. She's a real nice girl. Go on now, Leon. I'm gonna eat this ham. (*He exits. She waits a moment then begins messing the food around on her plate. Collard enters from the front door. She has changed into one of Leon's shirts and a pair of rolled up jeans. She has washed her face, but her hair is still a mess.*)

COLLARD. Hi.

MARSHAEL. Hi. Get the kids off okay?

COLLARD. Oh, sure. Aunt Muffin had frozen coca colas waiting for them and she's letting them watch TV till ten o'clock.

MARSHAEL. That's good.

COLLARD. (*Getting a cigarette from the carton that she has brought in with her.*) Oh shit, you know I forgot t'ask Aunt Muffin if I could borrow something of hers for the funeral. Jesus, I'm so unreliable it's almost perfect.

MARSHAEL. Oh, well. Never matters. We'll make do. So did the children really enjoy the ride over in the convertible?

25

COLLARD. Sure. I'll say. Lucy had a sack full of rocks she kept throwing out at cows as we passed by. She said she hates cows now and she wants to kill them all! I love that child. She reminds me of me.

MARSHAEL. Well, I hope she didn't hurt any of the poor animals.

COLLARD. Oh, no. Missed 'em by a mile. She just had to blow off steam, that's all. Don't blame her for that. Some miserable day, huh?

MARSHAEL. Sure was.

COLLARD. Lordy, Lord.

MARSHAEL. Katty kept going around pretending like we were giving some sort of ghastly tea party. "Here's a coaster and a fresh napkin for your drink. Do you need some more ice cubes? Oh, by the by, the deceased is residing in the parlor."

COLLARD. He's the one in the yellow plaid coat.

MARSHAEL. Agony, agony, agony.

COLLARD. Course now, Katty is a Windsor form North East Jackson. That makes her real quality folk.

MARSHAEL. Did you see the way Willie Wayne started tap dancing around when her daddy and uncles arrived to pay their respects?

COLLARD. I expected him to start passing out his business cards at any moment.

MARSHAEL. The thing I love about Willie Wayne is I can just totally despise him.

COLLARD. She's got him monogramed from top to toe— wearing those three piece business suits—

MARSHAEL. Don't forget his genuine cow leather brief-case—

COLLARD. He's moving up at the bank—

MARSHAEL. He ain't trash no more!

COLLARD. Speaking of trash—

MARSHAEL. Who?

COLLARD. Mother Foster and her humpbacked brother!

MARSHAEL. Please! If I hear the tale about—

COLLARD. What?

MARSHAEL. How she was just like her brother, Wilbur, had a hump growing in her back—but she prayed to God and He straightened up her back and at the same time made all her dandruff disappear.

COLLARD. Oh, no!

MARSHAEL. Yes!

COLLARD. What are you drinking?

MARSHAEL. Gin.

COLLARD. Where's the bottle? (*Suddenly a loud commotion is heard coming from the kitchen off L. Smoke comes pouring in from the kitchen. As she exits R.*) What the hell is that? What's all this smoke? (*Marshael takes a sip of her drink, Wayne enters in an uproar from U.C.*)

WAYNE. She's a firebug, a menace, a pyromaniac lunatic! (*Katty follows him into the room.*)

KATTY. Hush up! Hush up!

WAYNE. I don't wonder she's a third degree burn victim!

KATTY. Will you please hush up!

MARSHAEL. What happened?

KATTY. Nothing. Little grease fire in the kitchen.

WAYNE. I haven't even finished my dinner. That smoke'll never clear!

KATTY. (*Calling off L.*) Just bring your plates on in here! We'll eat in here! The dining room table's already set for tomorrow's buffet! (*Pixrose and Leon enter carrying their supper plates.*)

WAYNE. And she stays out of the parlor! There's flammable material in there. She stays away from it!

PIXROSE. I'm so sorry. I'm so sorry. I'm so sorry.

LEON. (*Overlapping.*) It's nobody's fault. That rag just burst into flames. Why it's no more your fault—(*Katty exits to the kitchen. Collard enters with the bottle of gin and two red kitchen chairs.*)

PIXROSE. (*Overlapping; to Wayne and Marshael.*) I'll pay for all the damages. Here, you can have my grandmama's garnet brooch. It's a priceless brooch. See—(*While trying to show the brooch, she manages to drop her plate and break*

27

it.) Oh, no! Oh, no!! Now my super plate is shattered! Look at the pieces! It's broken for life!

MARSHAEL. It's an old plate, Pixrose. For Heaven's sake! It doesn't even matter—

WAYNE. That girl is a menace! A total menace!

PIXROSE. (*Overlapping, as she tries to pick up the pieces.*) OH, oh, oh, oh, oh—

LEON. (*Overlapping.*) Look, here, you're making Pixrose unhappy! You're making her cry!! Don't cry!

PIXROSE. I'm just picking up the pieces. I've never been in people's homes.

COLLARD. Here, sit down, Pixrose. Sit down. Have some gin. Take a swallow.

WAYNE. Will somebody sit her down before she tears this place apart!? What's this I'm stepping on?! Looks like jelly beans! It's jelly beans! Oooh!! What next?! What next?!!

(*Wayne scrapes jelly beans off his shoes as Katty enters from the dining room with a tray of supper plates, glasses, etc.*)

KATTY. Here, everyone. We'll just finish our supper in here. We'll have a nice quiet supper in here. Oh, was there another accident?! For Heaven's sake!

MARSHAEL. It's all right, Katty—It's nothing at all. Just a stupid plate!

KATTY. Fine then. Just fine. Wayne, why don't you come sit down over here and finish your supper. (*Leon throws the broken pieces into a garbage can with a loud crash. There is a long moment of silence.*) I heard a very interesting piece of information this afternoon. (*Leon surreptitiously throws an English pea at Wayne. Wayne looks around.*) Mattey Bowen informed me that when you're buying canned stewed tomatoes the cheapest brand is actually preferable to the most expensive. (*Leon throws another pea at Wayne.*) You see, those cheaper brands move off the shelves at a much faster rate, and, therefore, they're the fresher product. (*Leon throws a third pea.*)

WAYNE. Are you throwing food at me? (*Leon throwing*

a pea at him.) He's throwing food at me! (*Leon slings a pea.*) Look at this! English peas! (*Leon is now openly throwing peas.*)

KATTY. Leon, really!

WAYNE. You'd better stop that! He'd better stop that! I mean it, by God!

COLLARD. For Heavens sake, Willie Wayne, it's just vegetables!

WAYNE. I don't care! I won't have it! This is a serious night! Give me that plate!

KATTY. (*Overlapping.*) Leon, please!

COLLARD. (*Overlapping.*) I don't believe he's having a conniption fit about a few vegetables!

WAYNE. I'll jerk you bald headed, boy! Give me that plate!

LEON. (*Throwing the rest of his food in Waynes's face.*) Here! I'm finished anyway. I cleaned my plate!

WAYNE. (*Taking the plate.*) What a brainless imbecile! I'm surprised they don't send him off to the moon!

LEON. He's always disliked me, ever since I was alive.

WAYNE. It's no surprise to me that you've never held down a job—have to live in a shack—

KATTY. Hush, now, honey—

WAYNE. Goes around picking up trash just for the fun of it. It near t'killed him when they brought out those no deposit bottles—cut his income clean in half. Isn't that so, Leon?

KATTY. Hush up, now, Wayne, darling. Leon has himself a permanent job now. Don't you dear?

COLLARD. Well, now, that's just wonderful.

WAYNE. First I've heard of it.

COLLARD. So, what do you do?

LEON. I work over at the chicken factory. I'm a turkey jerker.

COLLARD. A what?

LEON. A turkey jerker. They send them old turkey carcasses by on this conveyor belt, and I jerk out the turkey innards and put 'em in a sack. Have me an apron I wear and everything.

WAYNE. Classic! That is too classic! Suit the man to the job, that's what I always say! Make a turkey jerker out of a jerky turkey! Classic! (*Leon is hurt.*)

COLLARD. Oh, cute, Willie Wayne. You've always been so cute. Remember how cute Willie Wayne used to be when we'd wrap him up in white surgical bandages—make him into a mummy and roll him down the hill? He made the best damn mummy!

PIXROSE. How could he breathe?

WAYNE. For a girl who flunked out of Co-lin College you're awfully smart. Course everyone knows Collard is a real live genius. Her and her high IQ.

MARSHAEL.	COLLARD.	KATTY.
Just, please, don't start—	Yes, we all have beautiful histories —Don't we now?	Now, if we can't say something nice, let's not say anything at all.

MARSHAEL. Owww!!!

LEON. What?

MARSHAEL. I bit down on that damn sore in the side of my mouth.

KATTY. Anyway, we've got all sorts of pressing issues to debate. For instance, we've got to make a decision about who all is going to ride out to the graveyard tomorrow in the limousine.

COLLARD. What limousine?   LEON. I hired it. (*The phone begins to ring.*)

KATTY. I'm sorry to have to bring it up, but Mother Foster is very concerned about it.

KATTY. Will you be a papa sweet potato and get that?

WAYNE. All right.

LEON. Why does she talk to him in that funny voice? (*Collard shrugs. Wayne answers the phone.*)

WAYNE. Hello . . . Hi, mama, what's going on?

KATTY. (*Overlapping.*) Now Mother Foster and you and Wayne and I are supposed to all ride out in the limousine, but Mother Foster sincerely desires for James Jr. to ride along with us.

LEON. I'm going to get those Rice Krispie bars out from the kitchen. (*He exits U.C.*)

KATTY. (*Running on.*) She feels although he is the youngest of the children, he is the only son and Jamey's namesake. (*Collard gets up and pours some more gin.*) Of course, I don't mind where I ride. It makes no never mind to me. But Mother Foster just thought— (*To Wayne.*) Who was that, darling?

WAYNE. Mother Foster.

KATTY. What'd she want?

WAYNE. Ah, well, it seems that, ah, Uncle Wilbur split some gravy on his good suit; so, ah, he'll need to get something of Jamey's to wear tomorrow. Mama says they're close to the same size in a lot of ways.

KATTY. Well, I'll pick something out for him. Marshael's been real busy.

WAYNE. She, ah, said she'd prefer the blue-pin-striped suit. I don't know which one she means.

MARSHAEL. Well, it's okay. I know which one it is.

WAYNE. (*Uncomfortable.*) And she mentioned something about you picking out a few suits for Uncle Wilbur to take on back up to Tubler with him tomorrow; seeing as, well, as you won't have much future use for them.

MARSHAEL. Whatever she wants. I've no objections.

WAYNE. She's a very practical old bird.

COLLARD. Sure and there's some silverware in the sideboard and coffee in the cupboard while she's at it!

WAYNE. Look, don't make fun of my mama.

COLLARD. Why not?

WAYNE. It's just too easy to poke fun at a poor, old farm woman who had to move down here and sell mattresses just so her two small boys could eat. (*Collard makes like she's crying.*) Oh, sure, she's just some red necky hick to you! But what makes y'all so high and mighty? Just 'cause your father was some drunken lawyer. You never learned a damn thing!

31

Why just look at the way this funeral is being run. I've never stood and witnessed such a tawdry affair in all my born days. (*Leon enters with a plate of Rice Krispie bars.*)

LEON. Who sent the Rice Krispie bars? They sure are good!

WAYNE. Why look at him!! He's got Jamey wearing a plaid sports jacket, for Christ's sake! It's—it's a mockery to decorum!

LEON. You don't like that jacket? I thought it was cheerful.

WAYNE. A red nose is cheerful! And that coffin in there! It is a disgrace! You may as well of sent off for a mail order job, or just picked up a couple of orange crates over behind the A & P! What could have possessed you, Marshael? What in the world could have possibly possessed you?

COLLARD. Well, what with all the insurance and savings and trust funds Jamey left her—

WAYNE. I'm not talking about that! Why the way you've refused to go in that room all day long shows me how ashamed you are of the way Jamey's been laid out on display —looking like some penniless clown in a box.

MARSHAEL. (*Rising to her feet.*) Willie Wayne, I'm getting awfully tired of listening to you talk—I'm getting awfully sick and tired of listening to one white man talk!

KATTY. Reverend Rigby says we all have to learn to face our own finiteness—

MARSHAEL. I mean all this sudden deep show of concern and respect when you never even liked Jamey! You never even cared for him at all. It made you happy watching him struggle and fail!

WAYNE. It never did—

MARSHAEL. I remember clearly how you gloated with joy last Christmas Eve giving us that colored TV set when all we could to give y'all was a double book of Life Savers! You never wanted him to succeed! You never wanted him to make good!

WAYNE. I never wanted! Hey, listen, Missy, you're the one who saddled him with those three children and that job he despised. You're the reason he never got his damn Master's degree.

32

MARSHAEL. Don't you talk to me about his Master's degree! You could have lent him the money. When I came to you—
WAYNE. I wanted to talk to him, not to you. It was a business arrangement! I needed to talk to him!
MARSHAEL. You needed to humiliate him! You needed to make him beg and plead and give up his pride!
WAYNE. What pride? You destroyed any pride he ever had! Why, by the time you were finished with him he was nothing but a broken alcoholic slob!
MARSHAEL. What the hell do you know about anything?
WAYNE. I know about you sneaking his incompleted manuscript off to that New York publisher and them telling him it was superficial and sophomoric and what were some of those other adjectives they used?

COLLARD. How 'bout noxious, putrid, stinking, balless, rotten, lousy junk? And I never even read it!
MARSHAEL. I had to see. I needed to see.

WAYNE. (*Continuing after a moment's pause.*) I don't blame him for walking out on you, after you showed him that letter! I don't blame him for that at all!! It was cruel and vicious and mean!

MARSHAEL. (*Continuing.*) I couldn't let us keep on lying and hoping. It was like slow poison! I never wanted him to leave. I didn't mean for him to leave.
WAYNE. Besides, I wanted him to have that TV set! I didn't care what he gave to us. We enjoyed those Life Savers. We did. (*There is a tense pause.*)
KATTY. Look, I—I brought my Sunday school pamphlets with me and my Bible and my Bible dictionary. Whatever you'd like to use.
MARSHAEL. I'm going upstairs. I'm tired. I'm going upstairs. I've gotta polish Lucy's shoes. I'm going upstairs. (*She goes up the stairs and walks into her bedroom.*)
WAYNE. (*After a moment.*) Anyway, he must have left her some money; some insurance.
COLLARD. Not a dog's dime.
PIXROSE. It says on this tag Mrs. R.K. Miller sent the Rice Krispie bars.

LEON. Are they your favorite dessert?

PIXROSE. So far.

LEON. They're mine too.

PIXROSE. It doesn't mean anything. 'Cept we like 'em.

WAYNE. (*About Marshael's plate.*) Look at this; she just messed the food around on her plate. She's thirty three years old and she's still messing the food around on her plate.

LEON. Pixrose is gonna be a dog bather when she graduates from high school. They've already got her placed at a dog hospital and everything.

KATTY. Well, how nice for you.

WAYNE. He was my brother. Of course you love him. She needs professional help.

LEON. Maybe I'll be moving up to Jackson and become her assistant or something.

PIXROSE. It's not that easy a job.

LEON. But I could do it. I could! I know I could! (*Pixrose gets up to leave the room.*) Where are you going?

PIXROSE. To watch the moon. (*Leon rises to go with her.*) By myself. (*Leon stops in his tracks, as Pixrose turns and leaves out the door.*)

LEON. I've loved her ever since we first met at Monkey Island.

KATTY. (*To Leon, who is on his way out.*) Where are you going?

LEON. To watch her watch the moon. (*He exits.*)

WAYNE. It's funny how, even after she showed him that rejection letter, he never stopped belittling my job at the bank.

KATTY. (*After a moment of silence.*) My. What a night. (*Pause.*) Well, the silences are all right too. Here, let me just clear these plates. (*She exits U.C. with some dishes.*)

WAYNE. (*About the gin.*) Do you mind?

COLLARD Never.

WAYNE. (*Pouring himself a glass.*) You know, even without combing your hair, you're still very pretty. (*Collard looks at him. There is a knock at the front door.*) Who do you think—

COLLARD. I don't know. (*Wayne opens the door for Brocker Slade. Brocker Slade, 53, enters holding a beat up hat in his hands and wearing a ten year old brown suit that he seems to be breaking out of. He carries two wooden spoons in his coat pocket. Brocker is big, tired, and worn out. Yet sometimes when he smiles, he will look like a confused child.*)
WAYNE. Yes?
BROCKER. Evening, I'm Brocker Slade. I hear you're having a wake.
WAYNE. Oh, yes, well, please do come in. I'm Wayne Foster, the younger brother of the deceased. And, ah, this is Collard Darnell. She's the sister to the widow.
BROCKER. Mighty pleased to make your acquaintence.
COLLARD. (*Immediately attracted.*) Likewise, I'm certain.
WAYNE. Perhaps you'd, ah, like to pay your respects?
BROCKER. Oh . . . yeah.
COLLARD Here, I'll show Mr. Slade to the parlor. I've yet to pay my own respects.
WAYNE. Why don't you then—
COLLARD. (*Taking her ham sandwich and drink with her.*) This way, Mr. Slade.
BROCKER. Brocker's fine.
COLLARD. Brocker then. (*They go into the parlor. Trying to avoid looking at the coffin.*) He's over there.
BROCKER. I see. (*Collard moves away from the coffin and eats a bite of her sandwich. In the hallway Wayne's drinking gin. Upstairs Marshael spins the world globe around. She stops it with her finger.*) So you're Marshael's sister?
COLLARD. Right. I don't live in this part of the state any longer. Generally, I just get back home for deaths; and Christmas occasionally.
BROCKER. Oh.
COLLARD. I don't like to affiliate myself with the rest of of this menagerie (*Upstairs Marshael looks at her violin. Katty enters the front hall from U.C.*)
KATTY. (*As she stacks the dishes onto a tray.*) Where's Collard?

35

WAYNE. In the parlor

KATTY. Oh, really? Well, at least she finally decided to go in!

WAYNE. Ah well, some visitor's in there with her—a Mr. Slade.

KATTY. No! Not that horrible man whose pigs all exploded.

WAYNE. (*Totally in the dark.*) I don't know.

KATTY. That old man who painted Marshael's kitchen chairs red. Terrible man—He told little Lucy she was an animal. She cried all day because of it.

WAYNE. (*In an annoyed whisper.*) Talk a little louder, why don't you?

KATTY. I'm sorry—But he's a barbarian, an absolute barbarian. (*She exits U.C. with the tray.*)

WAYNE. (*Whispering after her.*) Twat.

BROCKER. (*Staring at the corpse.*) Wonder why she married him? I do. I often wonder why.

COLLARD. Did you know him?

BROCKER. Met him when I moved here 'bout two years ago. Saw him off and on; here and there.

COLLARD. What'd did you think of him?

BROCKER. He appeared to me to be a miserable, bewildered man.

COLLARD. I never liked him. He had a genius IQ and all the promise in the world, but he was a lazy coward with no guts and never finished a thing he'd start. He lied to himself and to everyone else.

BROCKER. Still he had that woman.

COLLARD. Oh, he deluged her with gifts and things when they were young. Bought her barbecued chicken every Saturday night. And he could tell stories and paint up dreams real pretty. She was sincerely mad for him. (*Setting her drink down.*) Oh, hell, I may as well have one last look at the son of a bitch. (*She moves up to the coffin carrying her ham sandwich. Totally amazed.*) God. When did he get so fat? He's downright fat.

BROCKER. Beats the hell out of me.

COLLARD. And his glasses. They've got him wearing his glasses. Oh— (*A piece of her ham falls onto the corpse.*)

BROCKER. Watch out here. (*Picking up the ham slowly, and offering it to her.*) You dropped some ham.

COLLARD. I don't want it.

BROCKER. (*After a moment of indecision.*) Ah, hell. (*He eats it. Katty enters U.C. with a dish rag.*)

KATTY. Wasn't it sweet of Uncle Ben and Uncle Walter to make the trip up from Jackson?

WAYNE. Yeah.

KATTY. (*Wiping up crumbs.*) Uncle Ben likes you alot. He said you were very poised. His opinion means a lot at the bank. Better move that glass, the napkin's soaked through and through.

WAYNE. Stop acting like my mother.

KATTY. What?

WAYNE. You remind me of my mother.

KATTY. (*Hurt.*) Oh. (*She goes back to cleaning.*)

COLLARD. Well, shit.

BROCKER. Huh?

COLLARD. If this fool can get through dying, anyone should be able to do it. I mean, look, here—he's doing it right. No questions asked. Shit, so what's the big deal?

BROCKER. I'd like t'know. (*Leon racing into the front hall.*)

LEON. Hi! Where's Brocker? Is he here? I saw his dog out back—

WAYNE. He's in the parlor.

LEON. Great! I'll go get Marshy—(*He starts up the stairs.*)

BROCKER. Think we've been in here long enough?

COLLARD. Sure. (*She goes to get her glass.*)

KATTY. (*Quietly to Wayne.*) If we only could have a child. You'd see I had so much to give.

LEON. (*Knocking at Marshael's bedroom door.*) Marshy. Hey, Marshael—

MARSHAEL. (*Still holding her violin.*) Yeah?

LEON. (*Opening her door.*) Come on downstairs. There's

someone here to see you.

MARSHAEL. Leon, I'm done in here—

LEON. Please, I know you'll be glad to see him. It'll ease your mind.

MARSHAEL. Who is it? (*Downstairs, Collard and Brocker move into the front hall.*)

LEON. You'll see; come on; please—

MARSHAEL. (*Moving to the upstairs landing.*) It better not be—(*Spotting Brocker.*) Brocker Slade.

BROCKER. Hi M. It's good to see you.

MARSHAEL. Well, I guess, you don't mind coming here tracking mud all over my feelings.

LEON. What's wrong?

BROCKER. Look, I came here for the wake. I hope to be of some meager help.

MARSHAEL. Help?

KATTY. She's upset 'cause he let her children eat Gravy Train. He told little Lucy she was an animal.

BROCKER. For God's sake, lady, she is an animal! The kid's a mammal!

KATTY. See! He's crazy!

MARSHAEL. (*Coming down the stairs.*) Look, Brocker, there is no reason to concern yourself with my vulgar travail; so just take that flea bitten mongrel of yours and get off a my place.

BROCKER. Hey, now, M. I'm telling ya I'm sorry about that night but frankly—

MARSHAEL. Go home, Brocker! I'm telling you to go home!

BROCKER. No ma'am, I'm staying here tonight. I'll sleep in a ditch; but I'm not leaving here, not till the last dog is dead. (*Pixrose enters U.C. with a pie.*)

PIXROSE. Marshael, a lady just brought over this pie for you. She says it's bluebarry.

MARSHAEL. What lady?

PIXROSE. A yellow haired lady.

MARSHAEL. (*Standing on the middle of the stairs.*) Give me that pie.

WAYNE. Don't give her the pie.

MARSHAEL. It's my pie. Bring it here.

KATTY. Look, I'll just take the pie—

MARSHAEL. Don't you dare take that pie!

WAYNE. Won't you please just—let me take the pie.

MARSHAEL. Give me that Godamn blueberry pie!! (*Pixrose takes the pie to Marshael.*)

WAYNE. Go on and give her the pie.

MARSHAEL. (*Tearing off the card.*) "With deepest love and condolence, Esmerelda Rowland." She sent me one of her pies.

COLLARD. Who's Esmerelda Rowland?

WAYNE. Ssshush up.

MARSHAEL. (*Walking up and down the stairs.*) She actually went and sent me one of her pies. Course they must be pretty good. Jamey got awfully fat eating them. Why, he must of put on twenty-five pounds in just four months they were living together.

COLLARD. Jamey was living with another woman?

MARSHAEL. You didn't know? Why it's been noised all over Madison County—Jamey Foster and his twenty-two year old, twice divorced, yellow haired, sweet shop baker!

COLLARD. I never heard.

MARSHAEL. (*Still pacing.*) Oh, sure, she was right out there in the field with him on the fatal night of his demise. So, who wants some pie? Who wants a big piece of blueberry pie? It's Jamey's favorite kind! It oughta be really good!

WAYNE. Come on, now, put the pie down.

MARSHAEL. (*Running to the top of the staircase.*) You'd better eat some. You'd better it all! I mean it now—

WAYNE. Come on, now, and give it to me—Marshael, just calm down and hand me that pie.

KATTY. Your nervous system's just all shocked—

MARSHAEL. (*Screaming as she waves the pie back and forth and over her head.*) Ooooooh!! Oooooooohhh!!

PIXROSE. (*Overlapping.*) She's gonna smash it.

KATTY. It's all so trying. Why, Reverend Rigby always says—

COLLARD. (*Overlapping.*)

the scream.) No, she's not— BROCKER. (*Overlapping.*) Oh, Lord, she's hot as a fire-cracker now!

MARSHAEL. (*Throwing the pie from the upstairs landing down to the floor below.*) You shitty pie!!

COLLARD. She did it! WAYNE. All over the rug!

PIXROSE. She sure did! KATTY. Look at that mess!

MARSHAEL. (*Totally still.*) I don't know how I'm gonna get through this night.

LEON. I never seen her scream out like that.

MARSHAEL. I can't imagine ever seeing the morning. (*The lights fade to blackout.*)

END OF ACT ONE.

ACT II

Scene 1

The setting is the same. The blueberry pie has been cleaned up. Marshael and Pixrose are upstairs in the bedroom. Marshael is working on one of the drill team costumes that is on the dress dummy. She wears the same black dress that she wore throughout Act one. Pixrose is dressed in a long cotton nightgown. She is polishing a small black patent leather shoe. Downstairs, Wayne is sitting at the card table that has been cleared. He is studying a camera and its flash attachment. He is also drinking gin. Leon is pacing back and forth in the front hall. From time to time he glances into the parlor to look at the casket that has now been closed.

LEON. (*After several moments of pacing.*) We just stand here? Is that all there is to it? This is it? This is a wake?
WAYNE. That's right.
LEON. Well, then I gotta go get me a drumstick! (*He exits U.R.C.*)
PIXROSE. Marshael, I've finished the first coat on Lucy's shoe. I'm gonna set it down here by Jamey Jr.'s and do the other one while it dries. (*She puts the shoe down on a sheet of newspaper and starts on the second one.*)
MARSHAEL. You're a big help. I appreciate it. (*The phone rings. Marshael starts.*) God, I hate it when that phone rings. It scares me. (*She picks up the phone.*) Hello? . . . Well,

how're you doing? How're your sisters? . . . Well, that's good
. . . What? . . . Why sure I remember the cut-out bunny you
made at school—It's green, right? . . . Well, I don't know,
Jamey, Jr., maybe you could—just give it to someone else . . .
Sure . . . No, Daddy wouldn't mind . . . No, honey, he wouldn't
mind a bit. I'm sure . . . Well, that's a good idea. I know
Uncle Leon would just love it. It's an awfully fine bunny . . .
Alright then, you sleep tight and don't let the bedbugs bite.
I love you, boy. Bye, bye. (*She puts down the phone.*) My little
boy's calling. He's only six. Gee. Thank God he's not crying
or anything. That's the worst thing for me, watching my
children cry.
PIXROSE. That's exactly how I feel about my brother,
Franky. I can't bear t'watch him cry.
MARSHAEL. Oh, I didn't know you had a brother.
PIXROSE. Well, he's out at Ellisville.
MARSHAEL. Oh. I'm sorry.
PIXROSE. He does all right. They've got him wearing this
football helmet all day and all night just in case he starts
banging his head into walls. Seems he's got some sorta brain
damage.
MARSHAEL. Do you see him much?
PIXROSE. Once a year 'bout Christmas time I'll visit him
and take him his gift—soap on a rope. He loves the soap on
a rope to wear in the shower. But other than my brother,
Franky, I have nobody.
MARSHAEL. Well . . . how do you feel about Leon?
PIXROSE. I don't know. He's probably just in love with love,
and he's something of a misfit. Still we did kiss each other at
Monkey Island. No, it will never, never be.
MARSHAEL. Why do you say that?
PIXROSE. (*Putting the shoe down to dry.*) I'd just rather
keep him like a jewel in my mind. That way I will always
have him. (*Picking up the violin.*) My, this is a fine looking
instrument. Do you play it?
MARSHAEL. Sort of. Jamey always left the house when I
started to play it though. He said it sounded screechy. (*Pixrose*

picks up the bow and plays a weird array of notes.)

PIXROSE. Sounds lovely t'me. (*Katty enters into the upstairs hall. She is wearing a pink robe and fluffy slippers. She
leans over the bannister and whispers down to Wayne.*)

KATTY. Psst, Papa Sweet Potato? Honey Pie? I've laid out
all your night clothes for you, if you decide you want to
retire.

WAYNE. (*Looking up at her.*) Why do you talk to me in
that funny voice?

KATTY. (*Stung.*) I don't know. I just do. Excuse me, I've
got to go and floss my teeth.

WAYNE. You sure do keep yourself clean. (*Katty hears
this last jab as she exits down the hallway. Wayne goes back
to drinking his gin.*)

MARSHAEL. (*After staring at the closet.*) Oh, well . . .
Lord. I'd better go on and get those suits out for Uncle Wilbur
while I'm thinking about it, leastwise I'll never do it. (*She
opens closet and gets his suits out.*) There. Here it is. His
blue pin-striped suit. I liked it best, and here I am holding it,
but somehow I don't feel a tear in this world. It's like a hole's
been shot through me, and all my insides have been blown
out somewhere else.

PIXROSE. Well, I know from my own experience that it
ain't ever gonna be worth it feeling all that love for somebody.

MARSHAEL. (*She gets a brush and starts brushing the suit.*)
Feeling love for somebody? I just wish I knew what I felt
for Jamey. First one thing, I guess, and then another, I sure
wish I knew. It haunts me not to know.

PIXROSE. Well . . . was he nice?

MARSHAEL. (*Continues to brush suit.*) He could be, I suppose . . . He did things different. I remember one time he
brought this huge, ugly, fat boy home with him about supper
time. Jamey whispered that he'd found the fat boy crying in
the road 'cause his only pet bird had flown away and could I
please fix blueberry muffins for dessert. He kissed my fingers
when I said I would. (*Cross to hall door—hang up suit.*) He
had dreams though. And it's hard being involved with a man

43

whose dreams don't get fulfilled.

PIXROSE. What dreams did he have?

MARSHAEL. Oh, he wanted to be a great world-wide historian. He used to have all sorts of startling revolutionary ideas about the development of mankind that he kept trying to write into books and theories.

PIXROSE. Well, he must a been a real smart man.

MARSHAEL. Oh, he was. And fun too. Why the way he laughed was so big and so strong—like the world was going to crack open and there's be beautiful treasures all inside. We sometimes played this game where we'd spin this globe around. (*Spin.*) Saying like, "We're gonna go . . . there!" (*She yells out the name of the country her finger actually lands on.*) Or, "We're taking a banana boat (*spin.*) to . . . here!" (*She looks down and reads the name.*) Then we'd imagine how it would be when we arrived. (*Sits on chest.*) It was a fun game, but we stopped playing after he had to take that awful job in real estate. (*She spins the globe around and around. She stops the globe with her finger and says the name of the country it lands on.*) I was afraid to ask him for anything. I never wanted him to know how scared I was. I just kept on telling him how, until all his theories were finished and started selling, that real estate was fine with me.

PIXROSE. And real estate's when you sell other people's homes for 'em?

MARSHAEL. Right. Except he didn't sell much of anything. I wanted so badly for things to be right for us. My parents fought all the time when I was little. Yelling and crying in the night. I wanted a different kind of life; but it didn't work out.

PIXROSE. He started yelling at you?

MARSHAEL. Oh, all the time. Stupid things like, "This mayonnaise jar is too damn small! Don't you know you save more money with the large economy size!" Slam! Break the jar! It was ridiculous.

PIXROSE. You musta cried a lot.

MARSHAEL. Oh, yeah. It seemed the harder I tried the less

he cared. The more he blamed me and the children for his dreams not coming true, I thought maybe it would help, if we just knew one way or the other about his work. That's why I sent it off to the publisher. When he found out, he was gone. Went off to live with that fat yellow-haired woman. And now he's really gone. He's out of the whole deal; and I don't even know what we felt for each other. Stupid. Lord. My mouth aches. (*Collard runs into the outside area R., carrying two bottles of gin.*)

COLLARD. (*Calling off R.*) Hey! Hey, last one here's a rotten egg! You're a rotten egg, Brocker! A goddamn rotten egg! Marshy! Marshy!

MARSHAEL. (*Going out onto the balcony.*) What? Don't shout.

COLLARD. Look! We got it! We got a load of gin! Here, I'll throw ya up a bottle.

MARSHAEL. No!

COLLARD. (*Swinging the bottles around and around in a circle.*) You ready?! Get ready!!

MARSHAEL. Stop! Don't be stupid, Collard! It's gonna break!!

COLLARD. Right! (*She stops swinging the bottles.*) Don't be stupid. That's kind of hard for me, huh? What with my low IQ—my bovine mind!

MARSHAEL. Oh, please! Look, just come on up here.

COLLARD. Why? You don't need things from me. You handle it all yourself.

MARSHAEL. Oh, please, I can't tonight. My mouth hurts.

COLLARD. That's right! Don't talk to me! Just run off carrying the world on your lonely shoulders.

MARSHAEL. Look, Collard, don't you talk to me about running off! You're the one who ran off and left me to keep care of Mama the six months she was sick, and then later, when Daddy was dying, you were here just long enough to upset everyone, then you ran off again!

COLLARD. He didn't wanna see me! He didn't need my help and neither did you! Nobody asked me to stay, 'cause I'm just too stupid! Just too damn stupid to live!

MARSHAEL. Shut up saying you're stupid! I'm so sick of that excuse I could wretch up blood! Ooh!!! (*She goes back inside.*)

PIXROSE. What's wrong with Collard?

MARSHAEL. She thinks she's stupid. She took some idiotic test twenty years ago that said she was dumb, and she believed them; so I guess she must be dumb. I don't know. My eyes ache. I'm gonna go put a cold rag over them. (*She exits into the bathroom. Brocker enters, D.R. carrying a bottle of whiskey. He is shaken.*)

BROCKER. Where the hell were you going to, a fire?

COLLARD. I only wish.

BROCKER. You hit something in the road, you know?

COLLARD. When?

BROCKER. That's what that large thud was that bumped us five feet out of our bucket seats.

COLLARD. It was probably just some old armadillo or coon crossing the road.

BROCKER. Well, there's blood and fur all stuck to your front fender!

COLLARD. It's okay; I never liked having solid colored cars.

BROCKER. Well, you don't.

COLLARD. Have a drink, Brocker. Clam yourself down. What's the matter with you? Don't you like plowing up the fields, raising some hell, dancing with glee?

BROCKER. Look, love, I don't need crazy. I've had crazy. I'm an old man.

COLLARD. You look mighty appealing to me (*Moving in on him.*) I don't think much of men, ya understand, I just can't live without 'em.

BROCKER. Honey . . .

COLLARD. Look, I just want somebody who's fun and crazy and mean as me.

BROCKER. Well, I'm none of those.

COLLARD. What's the matter, Brocker, honey . . . you gonna leave me forever unravished?

BROCKER. Look, it's just I — I like Marshael. I mean, God help my feeble soul, but — I do.

COLLARD. Oh, Marshael. Right, Marshael. Well, that's all right then. 'Course she's nothing like me. She doesn't caress death and danger with open legs. (*She takes a long, slow slug of gin.*)

BROCKER. (*Not accusing.*) Are you really this tough?

COLLARD. No, darling, I'm pretending to be tough. But if you pretend really hard, it amounts to about the same thing. Here, now, I'll call your lady love out for you. Marshael! Hey! Come on out here! An old troll wants to woo you! (*Pixrose goes out on the balcony as Collard exits.*)

PIXROSE. What is it? Marshael's putting water on her eyes.

BROCKER. It's not a thing. Sorry for the disturbance. Go back to sleep.

PIXROSE. Hey, listen, you need to dip that skinny black dog of yours. He's practically more flea than dog.

BROCKER. I don't own that old junk yard dog. It's not my dog. I never feed it. I got no idea how it even stays alive— chews on the same damn piece of wood all winter long. It's not my dog. I got no use for it! (*Marshael comes out of the bathroom with a washcloth.*)

MARSHAEL. (*Moving out to the balcony.*) Who's that? Is that Brocker? Is that Brocker Slade?

PIXROSE. (*Moving out of the way.*) It is.

MARSHAEL. You lily-livered man! When I needed you where were you? I'm sick of betrayal! Sick!

BROCKER. Look, I'm sorry, M. I'm sorry about last Tuesday night, but I'm a fifty-three years old jackass, and I hadn't even kissed a woman in close on to two years—

MARSHAEL. You're no good, Brocker! No damn good! I don't even like laying my eyes on you.

BROCKER. God, M., honey, you're breaking my heart. I'm about ready to run jump into the Big Black River.

MARSHAEL. Well, don't forget to hang a heavy stone

around your scrawny old neck.

BROCKER. Lordy, lord, is there no redemption in your heart?

MARSHAEL. It's in mighty short supply.

BROCKER. What do you want from Me? What?

MARSHAEL. (*It comes to her.*) Triumph! It's a feeling I'm sadly lacking. Give me some triumph: some glory: some exaltation!

BROCKER. So what do you want me to do? Climb up the side of the house and carry you up to the moon on a cloud?!

MARSHAEL. Yes! Try it! At least you can try it!

BROCKER. I'd break my scrawny old neck!

MARSHAEL. Then why don't you use some ingenuity!

BROCKER. Ingenuity?! Hell! Here goes — (*He makes a feeble attempt to climb up the side of the house and falls back down to the ground.*)

MARSHAEL. You call this ingenuity?!

PIXROSE. He might make it, he might.

MARSHAEL. No, he won't, he'll never — ow!

BROCKER. What's wrong?

MARSHAEL. My mouth! Those sores!

BROCKER. Christ! Oh, my back!

MARSHAEL. You stupid old fool! Oh, I'm through with it! Through with it all! (*Marshael leaves the balcony and slams into the bathroom. Pixrose looks out on the ledge as Brocker gathers himself together.*)

PIXROSE. Hey, there's a bird's nest out here. It has little blue speckled eggs in it waiting to be born.

BROCKER. I'm falling on my butt for a woman with sores in her mouth. Hell, I think I'm gonna go 'round and kick that stupid dog till he dies! (*Brocker hobbles off as Collard enters the front door. The lights in the front hall are dim. Collard is brooding: her shoulders are slumped. She carries a bottle of gin under each arm.*)

COLLARD. (*To Wayne.*) Hello.

WAYNE. Hey, Collard. Say, could you come take a look at this camera? Have I got this on right? (*She walks over to the table. He hands her the camera.*)

COLLARD. Hmm. Sure, it's right. It's perfect. Now all you do is look through here and click this button and you'll have a pretty picture.

WAYNE. Thanks.

COLLARD. (*Setting a bottle of gin down on his table.*) Here's your gin.

WAYNE. Thanks, Charlotte.

COLLARD. Huh?

WAYNE. Charlotte. That's your name isn't it? I like it better than Collard. Charlotte. (*As he lifts her chin wth his fingers.*) It suits a certain side of you. Charlotte.

COLLARD.What are you doing?

WAYNE. Huh?

COLLARD. Lifting my chin up like that—you're making me feel like some sort of goddamn horse—I'm not a horse!

WAYNE. (*As he backs her against the red chair.*) You are a horse! A goddamn horse! Come here—come here—

CLOOARD. (*Overlapping.*) Oh, so you do like your women dirty?

WAYNE. (*Grabbing her.*) I like you—I like you—Charlotte! Oh, Charlotte!! (*They manage to knock a chair over as Katty appears on the upstairs landing. She is winding a clock.*)

KATTY. (*Coming down the stairs.*) What's this? Wayne? What's going on here?! Excuse me, please, but what's going on?! (*Leon enters U.R.C. with a plate of chicken.*)

LEON. You know, that green dish detergent really does feel softer on your hands . . . What's going on?

COLLARD. (*After a tense moment.*) Oh, Willie Wayne was just giving me extremely good chance at nothing.

KATTY. It is becoming more and more painfully apparent that you have no affection or regard for me, whatsoever!

WAYNE. Go on up to our room, Katty. We'll talk up there.

KATTY. Just because my daddy gave you a decent job there's no reason to resent me! (*Marshael comes out of the bathroom upstairs.*)

MARSHAEL. Who's fighting? (*Pixrose shrugs her shoulders.*

49

Marshael goes and opens the bedroom door.)

WAYNE. We'll discuss it all in our room—

KATTY. Just because I lose those babies is no reason to treat me viciously—No reason at all! You know I can't help it!

WAYNE. You're crazy now, Katty—Totally crazy!

KATTY. And I'm nothing like that redneck mother of yours! I wouldn't be caught dead wearing those broad, bright-colored stripes! Especially if I was as fat as she is!!

WAYNE. Go to our room, Katty! Now!

KATTY. I won't! I won't! I won't! (*Katty starts up stairs and rushes past Marshael into the bedroom.*)

MARSHAEL. Katty—(*Marshael follows her into the bedroom.*)

KATTY. (*Runs to bathroom.*) She should be wearing dark clothes with vertical stripes!! (*Katty slams the bathroom door shut and locks it. As she continues yelling she bangs her fists on the door.*) Everyone knows that!! Everyone!!!! Everyone but that stupid, fat, old redneck! (*Brocker opens the front door—shuts it—looks around at everyone.*)

BROCKER. (*Gesturing with his whiskey bottle.*) What'd I miss? (*The lights fade to Blackout.*)

END OF SCENE

ACT II

Scene 2

The lights go up on the bedroom. Three large Easter baskets are out around the room. Most of the candy from these baskets has been devoured. Pixrose is pulling through the green grass in one of the baskets look-

ing for more candy. Marshael is fooling with her violin and drinking gin. She still wears the black dress but has taken off her shoes and stockings. Collard is pounding on bathroom door.

PIXROSE. Look, here's another marshmallow chicken—who wants it?

MARSHAEL. I'll take it!

COLLARD. How long you think she's gonna stay in there? All night or what? Katty?! Hey, Katty!

KATTY'S VOICE. *(She speaks from inside the bathroom.)* Look, please, I'll be out soon. Really.

COLLARD. When? You've been in there over an hour and a half already. Now, when?

KATTY'S VOICE. Soon. I—I just can't come out now.

COLLARD. For Christ's sake, why not?

KATTY'S VOICE. I don't know. I'm too ashamed. I can't forget it. My life has ended. I can't forget it.

COLLARD. *(Turning back to Marshael and Pixrose.)* So what am I supposed to do, go down to East Peace Street and throw myself in front of cars or what?! Oh, shit! I'm just leaving then. Going back up the Natchez Trace and stop stirring up trouble for everyone here. What'd I do with G.W.'s boots? Where the hell are those stupid boots?

MARSHAEL. Oh, damn it, Collard.

PIXROSE. Oh, Collard, wait. Here, wait. Hey, Katty? Katty? This is me, Pixrose Wilson. And, well, I'm really sorry you're feeling so badly upset. But you just need to, ah— come on out a the bathroom.

KATTY'S VOICE. I just can't face it. I can't. Why, none of y'all have suffered the cruel humiliation I have. None of y'all.

PIXROSE. Oh, sure. We've all had cruel, sad, unbearable things happen to us in this life.

COLLARD. No kidding.

PIXROSE. Look, here's one just happened recently to me. It's when Laurie Crussy said she would set the Sacred Heart Orphanage Asylum on fire, if I wouldn't give to her my grandmama's garnet brooch which is my only cherished possession.

COLLARD. What?

MARSHAEL. Really?

PIXROSE. That's right and she did it too. Burned down two entire wings 'cause she knows how fiercely and dreadfully afraid I am of fires.

COLLARD. My God! That's awful! Did you tell someone? Did you report that little monster?

PIXROSE. Well, 'course I did, but old Sister Daniel said I told lies out of jealousy over Laurie's pink, satin skin. Now I know my skin is ugly, but it wasn't a lie. (*Moment of stunned silence.*) So Collard? What about you? Do you have one?

COLLARD. Yeah. Well . . . the one that keeps coming to my mind is about Daddy.

KATTY'S VOICE. What? I can't hear it?

COLLARD. (*Moving to the bathroom door.*) Daddy—our daddy—how I used to be his favorite. We'd always talk and discuss life and politics. He wanted me to come join his firm —be a lawyer with him. Then when I was twelve we took these stupid IQ tests. Mine, well, mine said I was below average; ninety-two or something.

KATTY'S VOICE. But Collard, honey, those tests aren't accurate. You should have taken it again.

COLLARD. I did. Twice more! It got lower each time! I ended up with an eighty-three. That's twenty-one points lower than Leon, for Christ's sake! Twenty-one points below Leon!! Oh, God! I was nothing in his eyes from then on! Just dumb and stupid and nothing! So, Katty, you coming out now?

KATTY'S VOICE. I don't know. I'm starting to feel better. Oh, I don't know.

MARSHAEL. Hey, Katty—I went to see Jamey Tuesday afternoon over at the hospital and Esmeralda was there. She was all dressed up in a flowered dress and a flowered hat. I didn't look very good; so I thought, "Well, I'll just say, Hello, and leave." But Jamey, he kept talking to me and making conversation and all the time he was holding Esmeralda's hand, or putting his arm around her waist to give it a squeeze. He said, "Hey, Marshael, why don't you try one of those delicious caramel pecan balls Essey brought? You could stand some weight on those saggy bones." It fiercely hurt me and my pride—like I wasn't even a woman.

KATTY. (*Coming out of the bathroom.*) Oh, Marshael, honey, you are a woman. A beautiful woman. Don't let anyone tell you different from that.

MARSHAEL. Oh, Katty. Katty. (*Then realizing.*) Katty!! You're out of the bathroom!!

COLLARD. Praise God! You're out!

PIXROSE. Bravo! (*Pixrose showers Katty with a handful of eggs in silver foil, as the lights go down in the bedroom and come up in the front hall below. Wayne is sitting on the stairs drinking and fooling with the camera. Brocker is sitting at the card table drinking the last of his whiskey. His sleeves are rolled up. You can see his tattoos. Leon is sitting, looking at a deck of dirty cards.*)

LEON. Wow! Great! Great! Hey, look Willie Wayne! Brocker's got a deck of playing cards with pictures of necked women on 'em! Well, well, some of 'em are wearing like aprons or tropical flowers, or looks like garden hoses—just take a look! They're spectacular!

WAYNE. Then *you* keep them. I'm gonna go and get those photographs taken for Mama. (*He goes into the living room.*)

LEON. Think he's still upset about his wife?

BROCKER. Who knows? He left his bottle though. I'll grab it while he's gone. (*He jumps up to get the bottle. The bones in his body crackle.*)

LEON. Gosh! Will you listen to all them bones cracking away under your skin!

BROCKER. Well, Christ. I'm an old man. What the hell do you expect?

LEON. Shoot. Yeah. So what's it like being old?

BROCKER. Pure D-shit. That's what. The highs are never

as high. The lows get lower. Hangovers'll last ya ten days. Your back aches; your butt hurts; you can't smell spring . . . Hey, how 'bout a game of Bid Whist?! (*Wayne returns.*)

WAYNE. I'll do it later. I'll get to it later, that's all. It's too dark in there now. Where's my gin?

BROCKER. (*Brocker holds up the bottle.*) Here.

WAYNE. Oh. Well, go ahead. Have a drink. Sure, help yourself. So, Mr. Slade, what's all this about pigs? I hear you, ah, raise pigs.

BROCKER. (*As he shuffles the cards and proceeds to deal out four hands.*) Right. That's right. I came down here for that distinct purpose. Came down here with a wild-haired, big-thighed woman—she's the one who supposedly knew all about this hog raising business. I was just backing her with my cash and affection, but, by the by, she runs off and leaves me holding the fuckin' bag. Seems we had some sort of run-in over a dog I'd kicked. She leaves me out in that old shack saddled with twenty-seven hogs. Only three of which remain, a good fifteen of 'em having exploded, the other nine got loose or died mysteriously. Hey, do you play Bid Whist?

WAYNE. Poorly.

BROCKER. Have a seat. Now we've got this one extra hand to deal with . . . hell, I'll just bid 'em both. No problem. (*They start picking their cards up.*)

WAYNE. So what about these hogs exploding? Was it a munitions accident, or what?

BROCKER. Hell no. They just got bigger and fatter, and, of course, they were eating like pigs, and one day their bellies would be dragging along the ground, and the next day their skin would be all stretched out and they'd explode and die.

WAYNE. Jesus. Amazing. This man's amazing.

BROCKER. Well, before it was all over I discovered a good many of 'em had these deformed damn butt holes and that was the major cause of it all. I mean, it certainly was the crux of it. Hey, Leon! Your bid, boy! Your bid! (*The lights black out downstairs and go up on the women in the bedroom.*)

KATTY. (*Pulling at her hair with glee.*) Oh, it's so awful!

54

It's too horrible! You won't think I'm sweet anymore!

COLLARD. We don't care! We don't care!

PIXROSE. No, we don't care! Tell us!

KATTY. Oh, all right. See, I was always rich, you know, and people always hated me for it. And one Easter Sunday I was walking to church with my maid, Lizzie Pearl. Well, I was all dressed to kill for in my white ruffled dress and my white Easter bonnet and carrying my white parasol. Well, we had to pass by the Dooleys' house, and the Dooleys were always known as white trash, and that bunch really despised me.Well, Harry and Virginia Dooley came up and shoved me down into a huge mudhole, spoiling my entire Easter outfit! I cired, I tell you, I cried!

COLLARD. For God's sake, Katty! This is supposed to be a story about the cruelest thing *you've* ever done, not that's been *done to you!*

KATTY. I haven't finished yet! Will you let me finish! See later on in the day, when the Dooleys were all in for their dinner, Lizzie Pearl and I sneaked back over to their back yard and yanked the chirping heads off of every one of their colored Easter chicks—We murdered them *all* with our bare hands! Those brats cried for weeks! I swear it was weeks!

COLLARD. Great! Katty, that's rotten. That is really rotten!

PIXROSE. (*Overlapping.*) Yes, that's cruel, Katty! That's very cruel!

KATTY. I know, that's why I told it. Who's got one now? Collard, I bet you've got one. I bet you do.

COLLARD. Oh, yeah—I've slept with married men, I've slept with priests, I've stolen from stores, I've killed animals in the road, lied and cheated just to win at a game of cards.

PIXROSE. Oh, but what I did was worse than that.

COLLARD. Yeah?

PIXROSE. See, after I was burned and had to be in bandages, I bandaged up all my dolls, put methiolade on the bandages and kept 'em down in the cellar. I kept 'em wearing slings and using crutches and some of 'em were even blind. See, just 'cause I was scarred, I wanted them to be too. It was not fair.

MARSHAEL. Well, listen to this one. After Jamey'd had that stroke and the left half of his body'd gotten paralyzed, I went into see him, and he asked me to bring him some of his papers from home. I told him he'd have to hobble home on his good side and get them himself 'cause I'd just sold our car t'pay for these ridiculous hospital bills. That's the last night I ever saw Jamey. He'd always made me feel so ashamed for being stronger and for getting our house and feeding the kids. Well, now he was gonna be weaker and more dependent than ever and I just wanted him t'pay for it.

KATTY. Oh, Marshael, I know Jamey was grateful to you for all the help you gave him.

MARSHAEL. No, he hated me for it. 'Cause when I left he said to me, "Fine, then when I die you just stick me in a pine box. Don't you dare go making five hundred drill team suits so that you can bury me in something nice, 'cause I won't be taking any more favors from you."

COLLARD. If Jamey didn't want your damn favors, he shouldn't of taken them.

MARSHAEL. No, 'cause after his work never came to anything again and again, we both got to resenting each other so bad. It seemed like the house and the children became mine and something else was his. It wasn't always awful but somehow it got to be. I don't know when it changed. I don't know when we changed. But I still remember the first time he said he loved me 'cause we were lying under the purple trees. (*The lights slowly fade out in the bedroom then go up immediately in the hall below. The men are all drunk. Brocker is playing the spoons. Leon is making loud, weird sounds. Wayne is singing a sad song.*)

LEON. OOH AHHH BREAKAAAAA!!!

BROCKER. (*Overlapping.*) Yes sir! Let the good times roll!

LEON. BREAKAAAWOOSHAA!!! Whoo! Sometimes I just like to make noises. Stimulates the old brain.

WAYNE. (*Coming out of some sort of stupor.*) You know,

people just get deader and deader each day they live!

LEON. (*Impressed.*) Wow. He's right. He's absolutely correct.

WAYNE. See I too can say sensitive, provocative things. Sir Jamey is not the only one among us with a brain which is what my dear Mama would have us all believe.

BROCKER. My dear old Mamee!

WAYNE. Get this. Get this! I'm pulling in fifty-five thousand bucks a year. Fifty-five thousand, and she's telling me how Jamey's the smart one, the creative one, the special one; and I'm just good in arithmetic! Just good in arithmetic, too classic! And now—now she wants me to take some farewell pictures of Saint Jamey so she can build him up a goddamn shrine! Well, screw her pictures! Screw her! and screw that stinking bastard in there!!! (*His nose begins bleeding.*) God, my nose. My nose. Lord Jesus! I've never known love. Never will. Oh, my nose. My nose. (*He exits U.C.*)

LEON. (*After a moment.*) People get deader and deader every day they're alive. That's deep.

BROCKER. Hell, anything's deep if you think about it long enough. A man's best friend's his dog is deep if you give it any thought.

LEON. (*Realizing that a man's best friend is his dog, is deep.*) Yeah.

BROCKER. People are always saying, "Life is this!"—"Death is that!" They think they'll clear everything up for themselves if they can just hone it all down to a small twist of phrase. Poor idiots! (*The lights fade downstairs and go on upstairs. The woman have settled in under blankets, pillows, etc. They are all drinking gin. It is darker now. All but one of the lights have been turned off.*)

KATTY. (*As she rubs lotion all over her face, and arms.*) I hate the me I have to be with him. If only I could have the baby it would give me someone to love and make someone who'd love me. There'd be a reason for having the fine house and the lovely yard.

57

MARSHAEL. God. I wanted children so badly. I was like some giant sea turtle looking for a place in the warm sand to lay my eggs. I felt all fertile inside. I wanted a home and babies and a family. But Jamey never wanted all that. Still I really thought I had to have it. I really thought I did.

COLLARD. Not me. No way. No how. After my abortion I went out and ate fried chicken. Got a ten-piece bucket filled with mashed potatoes and gravy, coleslaw, and a roll. First it tasted good and greasy and gooey. Then I felt like I was eating my baby's skin and flesh and veins and all. I got so sick— all there in the car. Now I — I never eat chicken. I take the pill and use a diaphram too. It'll never happen again. (*Dipping a stick into a bubble jar. Waving her hand, making bubbles.*) Wooh, look at those . . . beautiful. (*She can't resist popping one.*)

PIXROSE. I've never actually been pregnant. I guess 'cause I'm, well, I'm still a virgin. But I was pregnant one time in a dream. And when the child was born he was half human and half sheep and they said he was to be sold as a slave. But before they took him, I was allowed to hold him in my arms. His body was so warm and soft. I felt his heart beating against my heart. Then I looked down at his small sheeplike face, and he was crying. Then they took him away to become a slave.

KATTY. (*She rises.*) Well . . . hum. We'll just be exhausted tomorrow. That's all there is to it, just totally exhausted. (*Twisting an alarm clock, heading for the door.*) Come on, Pixrose, I'll help you get settled into the children's room. Good night, all.

MARSHAEL. Katty. Ah, what are you gonna do tomorrow —'bout Willie Wayne and all?

KATTY. Why, nothing. That's all I can do. I don't have children or a career like you do. Anyway I don't like changes. My hair's still the same as I wore it in college. Come on, Pixrose, it's late. (*Pixrose and Katty leave the bedroom and exit down the hall.*)

COLLARD. God, I feel so old and tired.

MARSHAEL. It's late. You try and get some sleep. It'll be morning soon. (*The lights dim upstairs as they rise downstairs. Leon and Brocker are in a deep discussion. Brocker is playing with the wooden spoons.*)

LEON. It's strange.

BROCKER. I know.

LEON. I mean she used to sing and whistle all the time when you were around painting those kitchen chairs red

BROCKER. It's strange.

LEON. She loved listening to you playing them spoons.

BROCKER. Yeah. Hey, look, I've got a thought. Why don't we get those snapshots taken for Willie Wayne? Do him a favor? After all, he's a bleeding man.

LEON. You mean it?

BROCKER. Sure. We got flash cubes; what the fuck.

LEON. Fine with me (*As they move into the parlor.*) So anyway, what happened with Marshael? I mean, you used to could make her laugh. I asked you over here 'cause you knew how t'make her happy.

BROCKER. Look, Leon, I can't make my ownself happy; so how the hell am I gonna make her happy?

LEON. (*As he removes the lift lid from the coffin.*) Well, I just don't understand what could have happened between you two. (*Noticing the corpse.*) Boy, I wonder what it's like really being dead.

BROCKER. Don't look like much. Smile! (*He takes the picture.*)

LEON. So what about Marshael? Why does she hate you now?

BROCKER. (*He takes pictures through the following.*) Who knows. She, ah, called me to come pick her up from the hospital Tuesday night. We were driving home. It was raining. She was upset, but, ah, but she still looked, you know, good. And for some reason, I started telling her how the first time I'd seen her was, when she was playing her violin at the pancake supper. I said she looked like some sort of wild, frightened angel, ripping up that violin with her black eyes blazing. Then, ah, she started crying. She told me to pull the car over. I did. Well, I don't know. Nothing had ever happened, that way, between us before, and I felt funny with my tongue down her throat holding onto her hair. You know, with her husband there paralyzed in the hospital and with her all in distress. Seemed like maybe I was taking advantage of a situation or something; and so I left. I just took off. Walked home in the storm. Stepped in some goddamn horseshit, leaving her there in the car—alone—wanting somebody; needing something. God. What an asshole. Jesus, no wonder she hates me. (*Upstairs Marshael walks out onto the balcony.*) I leave the one woman I love alone in a great, unrelenting deluge. I give her nothing. Nothing. Not one thing. God, help us all. Listen, Leon; I gotta go. (*He heads for the front door.*)

LEON. Go where?

BROCKER. To find it. To get it.

LEON. What? To get what?

BROCKER. Exaltation! Love! Rapture! Glory! That's all there is! That's all that's left. (*He exits. As the lights go down, Leon returns to the parlor to put the lid back on the coffin. The moonlight drifts into the bedroom. Collard is sleeping in the bed. Marshael is standing on the balcony, talking to herself.*)

MARSHAEL. I won't sleep. My eyes are red I'm afraid to sleep. It's not like my nerves are raw, you know. It's like—like they've been stripped, leaving nothing but cold, cold bones. (*Pixrose enters the upstairs hall in her nightgown. She is terrified, distraught.*)

PIXROSE. I can't stay there. I can't. I can't.

LEON. Pixrose? What's wrong? Are you all right?

PIXROSE. I don't like sleeping in the children's room. All the toys and dolls look at me and scare me—

LEON. Here, now, here. Don't be scared. Don't be.

PIXROSE. See, it's not fair how my folks were trying to burn Franky and me up too. They were afraid of things. Thought life was evil and burned themselves up. But—but they shouldn't a tried burning me and Franky away with them.

First at home and then in that car. Still though, we survived. We survived—Oh, Leon. (*Then as she leaps down the stairs into his arms.*) Hold me quick!

LEON. Here, now, here. (*Leon picks her up in his arms. Then, after a moment, starts to carry her out.*) I'll get you a glass of milk. There's a cot on the back porch. You can drink the milk out on the cot. Out where Brocker's dog is sleeping. (*He carries her out through the dining room. The lights focus back on Marshael's room. She is talking to herself and putting Jamey's clothes in a sack.*)

MARSHAEL. All these ties. You never wore even half of 'em. Wasted ties. God, loose change. Always pockets full of loose change. And your Spearmint chewing gum sticks. Damn, and look—your lost car keys. Oh, well, the car's gone now. Damn you, leaving me alone with your mess. Leaving me again with all your goddamn, gruesome mess t'clean up. Damn, you, wait! You wait! You're not leaving me here like this. You're gonna face me! I won't survive! You cheat! I've got t'have something . . . redemption . . . something. (*She leaves the room, goes down to the parlor and walks in. The coffin is closed She begins to circle it.*) There you are. Coward. Hiding. Away from me. Hiding. (*Moving in on him.*) Look, I know I hurt you something bad, but why did you have to hold her fat, little hand like that? Huh? Treating me like nothing! I'm not . . . nothing. Hey, I'm talking. I'm talking to you. You'd better look at me. I mean it, you bastard! (*She pulls the lid off the coffin.*) Jamey. God, your face. Jamey, I'm scared. I'm so scared. I'm scared not to be loved. I'm scared for our life not to work out. It didn't, did it? Jamey? Damn you, where are you? Are you down in Mobile, baby? Have you taken a spin t'Mobile? I'm asking you — shit — Crystal Springs? How 'bout Scotland? You wanted to go there . . . your grandfather was from there. You shit! You're not . . . I know you're not . . . I love you! God. Stupid thing to say. I love you!! Okay; okay. You're gone. You're gone. You're not laughing. You're not . . . nothing. (*She moves away from the coffin, realizing it contains nothing*

61

of value.) Still I gotta have something. Still something . . . (*As she runs out of the parlor then out the front door.*) The trees. Still have the trees. The purple, purple trees— (*The front door is left open. There is a moment of silence before Brocker appears in the side yard carrying wild flowers and a ladder. He is very drunk. He wears some of the flowers in his hair.*)

BROCKER. Hey! Love! My, love! I'm carrying you off to the moon! To the starts! To the shining planet of Mars! (*He now has the ladder up and is making his way to the top.*) *Exaltation!!!* Where angels aspire to glory! *Exaltation!!!*

COLLARD. (*Overlapping, as she comes out of her sleep.*) Who's there? Shut up. My aching head. God! Who is it?! Stay away! (*She runs out onto the balcony and starts throwing colored Easter eggs at Brocker.*) Who's there? Stay away! Go away! I mean it. Get out of here! God. Take that.

BROCKER. (*Overlapping.*) Hey, love! I'm carrying you in my arms to paradise! Remember?! Exaltation?!! Hey, watch it! OW! Look out, that's my chest!

COLLARD. (*Running on.*) It's Brocker! You lunatic! You raving imbecile!

BROCKER. (*Overlapping.*) Collard, you bitch!

COLLARD. (*She is at the ledge now and throws the real eggs out of the bird's nest.*) Take that! You stinking drunkard! You broken dog. Take that!!

BROCKER. (*Overlapping.*) AAH!!! YUK!! Help! Help!

COLLARD. Oh, God! Look at this! Look! Now you've made me murder these baby eggs! I've done murder! What else is left? What else?! OOOHH!! (*She collapses back down onto the bed.*)

BROCKER. Jesus! YUK!!! It's a madhouse. There's nothing more but to go sleep in a ditch with my dog. Here, Pooch! Hey, Pooch! (*Brocker whistles. A dog's bark is heard in the distance.*) Pooch, come here — Pooch, Pooch! (*He walks off looking for the dog, as the lights fade to blackout.*)

END OF SCENE

ACT III

Scent 3

It is the following morning. The coffin and the flower arrangements have been removed. The blue pin striped suit is also gone. The visible rooms in the house are empty. Pixrose is outside. She wears a pink dress with long white gloves and white stockings. She has on a hat with cherries. She is humming a song and spinning around and around in circles as the lights go up. Brocker enters R. He looks like he has been sleeping in a ditch.

PIXROSE. (*Still spinning.*) Hi Brocker! Good morning!!
BROCKER. Yeah, morning. Hey, what's going on?
PIXROSE. Just spinning around! Trying to make myself dizzy—(*Laughing as she staggers to the ground.*) It's fun. You wanna try it?
BROCKER. No, thanks. I don't need to spin t'get dizzy any more. I'm just blessed with it.
PIXROSE. Hey, Leon and me washed your dog for you this morning.
BROCKER. (*Picking up the ladder.*) Well . . . thanks.
PIXROSE What's his name anyway?
BROCKER. He's called Blacky. That's his name, Blacky. (*Brocker walks away carrying the ladder as Collard comes out of the upstairs bathroom. She is dressed in an ill fitted dress with ridiculous shoes and a funny looking hat. The outfit should be the exact opposite of the image Collard likes to*

present of herself. She wabbles out of the bathroom and stares at herself in the mirror.)

COLLARD. You look perposterous. Absolutely and totally. I'm not going. That's all. I'm just not going. (*Leon and Katty enter from the dining room. Katty is dressed in her navy blue outfit. Leon has on his suit and tie. He carries a corsage and boxes containing the armbands and veils. He sets the boxes down on the card table.*)

KATTY. But did you see her at all this morning?

LEON. No, I ain't seen her at all.

KATTY. Are you sure she didn't go with Wayne to deliver the suit?

LEON. No, she didn't go with him. I spoke to him before he left—

KATTY. You did? What did he say? Was there anything interesting that was said? (*Wayne enters through the front door. He is dressed in a three piece suit.*)

WAYNE. Leon! Is she back? Has Marshael come back?

LEON. No, no one's seen her at all.

WAYNE. Well, we've got to find her!

LEON. Look, I gotta give Pixrose this precious rememberance. Marshael'll get back if she wants to. (*Leon exits to the kitchen. There is a tense moment of silence between Katty and Wayne.*)

WAYNE. I, ah, took Uncle Wilbur his suit.

KATTY. That's good.

WAYNE. Look, things have really been tense for me. Losing my only brother and all. It's been a shock.

KATTY. I know, Wayne, I know. Here, I'll ah, make some eggs up for you and heat the coffee. You gotta keep your strength up, Angel Pie. You know that? You really do. (*They exit through the dining room door, as Leon comes around the house, R., to find Pixrose sitting in the grass.*)

LEON. Hi.

PIXROSE. Hi.

LEON. You look pretty. That's a pretty dress . . . the hat too.

PIXROSE. Thanks. It's my Easter outfit.

64

LEON. Well . . . Here's a gift for you.

PIXROSE. For me?

LEON. Them's purple violets. It's my favorite kind of flowers. But—but that don't mean that they have to be your favorite kind too!

PIXROSE. They smell pretty. (*Holding the flowers up to Leon.*) Here, smell them. They're pretty.

LEON. Good. Hey, you wanna go 'round to the front and wait for the limousine? It's due to arrive directly.

PIXROSE. Sure! I've never seen a limousine before!

LEON. You think I have? (*They exit to the front of the house. Suddenly Marshael, Wayne, Katty and Brocker all enter the front hall from U.C. They are in an uproar. Marshael starts up the stairs; the rest follow her.*)

KATTY. Really, Marshael, I think, for your own sake, you should go —

BROCKER. (*Overlapping.*) Will you stop hounding the woman! For Christ's sake —

WAYNE. (*Overlapping.*) But you've got to go! You can't not go! Why won't you go?

MARSHAEL. Because I'm tired! I'm finally tired. I think I can sleep. And what's that horrible smell?!!

KATTY. I know! It's like — rotten eggs! What could it be?

WAYNE. But it's a disgrace, if you refuse to go to your own husband's funeral! A selfish, foolish disgrace! (*They are upstairs by now. Marshael enters her bedroom. The rest follow.*)

MARSHAEL. Look, I'm not going to go and put that rotting mess of formaldehyde in the ground, and that's all there is to it!

WAYNE. You're totally irreverant! Totally! There ought to be some sort of law —

BROCKER. (*Overlapping.*) The woman needs rest, you asshole!!

COLLARD. (*Overlapping.*) What's all this?! Don't bring *him* in here!!!

BROCKER. Oh, what do *you* know!

COLLARD. Lunatic!

65

WAYNE. (*To Marshael.*) Look, just comb your hair, and we'll go. It's getting late!

MARSHAEL. What's that rotting smell? It's making me sick.

KATTY. Collard, are you wearing that?

COLLARD. No! (*Suddenly Leon rushes in the front door.*)

LEON. (*Yelling up to them.*) Hey. Hey, everyone! It's here! The limousine! It's here! (*He runs back out and R.*)

WAYNE. The limousine?!

KATTY. Oh my, it's finally arrived. (*They start down the stairs.*)

WAYNE. Well, I'd better go check on it.

KATTY. Here, I'll go too. You might need some help.

WAYNE. Make sure things are all in order.

KATTY. Make sure they have the directions straight.

WAYNE. Make sure the headlights are all working. (*Katty and Wayne exit the front door.*)

MARSHAEL. It's you, Brocker. That smell; it's you.

BROCKER. I know it. I know.

MARSHAEL. Well, it's making me dizzy.

BROCKER. Sorry. Look, I'll go change. I'll just go change. (*He leaves the room and goes downstairs. In the front hall he starts to take his shirt off. He picks up his hat and coat and the two wooden spoons and then walks out the front door. It is all right if his actions overlap somewhat with the scene that is going on upstairs in the bedroom.*)

COLLARD. Look, Marsh, I can't go to the funreal. I just look too preposterous. I don't even have on clean underwear. I'm not gonna go.

MARSHAEL. But you gotta go. I—told the kids you'd go. I had breakfast with them over at Aunt Muffin's this morning. They wanna ride in the white convertible. They said they wanna ride with you.

COLLARD. But who are you gonna go with?

MARSHAEL. I don't need to go. Shit, Collard. I'm asking you to go!

COLLARD. (*A moment.*) All right then. I'll go. I'd be glad t'go

66

MARSHAEL. Good. I told them you'd bring their shoes when you came.

COLLARD. All right. Here, I can put 'em in here. God. You need rest bad, Marshy. Look here, your hands are shaking.

MARSHAEL. Right. Yes. I'm gonna try and get some sleep soon. Stop my eyes aching.

COLLARD. (*Picking up the children's shoes.*) Good then you rest. I gotta go. Don't worry. I'll see they get their little shoes. I'll take care of it all. You sleep. (*Wayne, Katty, Leon, and Pixrose all come in the front door. Pixrose is wearing the violet corsage.*)

WAYNE. I don't believe they've got Jersey Crow driving our limousine in that stupid hat.

COLLARD. That's them.

LEON. Look, if she doesn't want to go, I don't see why she should have to go. (*Handing Wayne a black arm band.*) Now here Willie Wayne, this is for you.

PIXROSE. Hey, Collard, look! Honeysuckle! (*She waves the honeysuckle to Collard who is coming down the stairs. Katty and Pixrose both start struggling with their veils. Katty is also putting on her gloves and getting her handbag.*)

WAYNE. Get Marshael, Collard, we've got to go immediately!

COLLARD. She's not going.

WAYNE. What is this? She's got to go! It's required!

COLLARD. Look, just because you'll always have the taste of leather in your mouth, doesn't mean the rest of us have to.

LEON. Collard, here's your veil.

PIXROSE. (*Overlapping.*) Am I wearing this right? (*Katty goes to her assistance.*)

COLLARD. (*Overlapping as she takes the veil with a new sense of command and warmth.*) Thanks. I'm gonna take the kids in the convertible. Look, you and Pixrose go in the limousine. (*She tries putting her veil on over her hat.*)

LEON. Great!

WAYNE. (*As he leaves.*) I wash my hands of it! I wash my hands of it entierly!

KATTY. Remember then, Collard. It's Grace Episcopal Church right on East Peace Street! Do you have that!

COLLARD. (*Putting her veil directly on her head then triumphantly putting the hat on over it.*) Yeah, I got it! I'll be there. I got it. (*They all exit out the front door. Upstairs Marshael rises. She has taken off her black dress and stands only in a white slip. She sits down on the bed and takes hold of a pillow. Brocker appears around the side of the house. He is wearing his hat and his dark suit coat without his shirt. He looks at the window, then starts playing a song on the spoons. Marshael wraps a blanket around herself and goes out onto the balcony.*)

MARSHAEL. Brocker—

BROCKER. Hi. Just dropped by. Thought you might need something. I don't know. Thought I'd see.

MARSHAEL. Thanks. I'm just gonna rest. Lord, you look awfully funny.

BROCKER. I do?

MARSHAEL. Sorta. What's that on your chest?

BROCKER. (*Opening his coat.*) A ship. (*Then making the ship move my moving his muscles.*) It's on a troubled sea.

MARSHAEL. (*Bursting out laughing.*) Oh, Lord! Look at that! A troubled sea!!

BROCKER. I like it when you laugh. I love to hear you laugh!

MARSHAEL. Really? I don't even know what my laugh sounds like.

BROCKER. It sounds . . . happy.

MARSHAEL. Hey, look, you could do one thing for me.

BROCKER. I could?

MARSHAEL. I need some more Easter candy for my kids. You know, things like bunnies and chickens and eggs and stuff.

BROCKER. Oh, sure, sure. I saw a whole bunch of that junk over at Ben Franklin's Dime Store. I'll, ah, get it for you right away. I'll buy a whole load of stuff! I'll run go and get it now! (*He starts to go R.*)

68

MARSHAEL. Brocker, wait! (*He stops.*)

BROCKER. What? What is it?

MARSHAEL. I don't know. Play something for me. Will you? Just till I go to sleep. Play something on the spoons. Would you?

BROCKER. All right. Sure. I'll play you a tune. Wanna hear, 'This Old Man?' I do it real well. Why—why you won't be able to keep your eyes open.

MARSHAEL. Play it. Yes, play that one. (*Brocker sits on the stump. He starts playing the spoons and singing "This Old Man."*)

BROCKER. (*Singing.*)
This old man
He played one
He played knick-knack
On my drum.
With a knick-knack paddy whack
Give a dog a bone
This old man comes rolling home.
This old man
He played two

MARSHAEL. That's nice.

BROCKER. (*Continuing.*)
He played knick-knack
On my shoe.

MARSHAEL. That's a nice song. (*She starts slowly into the bedroom.*)

BROCKER. (*Continuing.*)
With a knick-knack paddy whack
Give a dog a bone
This old man comes rolling home.

> MARSHAEL. (*Getting into bed.*) I like it.

This old man
He played three
He played knick-knack
On my knee

MARSHAEL. (*Almost a-sleep.*) I do... (*She falls asleep as he continues to play the spoons.*)

With a knick-knack paddy whack
Give a dog a bone
This old man comes rolling home.

This old man
He played four
He played knick-knack
On my door
With a knick-knack paddy whack
Give a dog a bone
This old man comes rolling home.

(*The lights fade to blackout.*)

PROP LIST

ONSTAGE
2nd LEVEL BEDROOM

On Bed
  2 throw pillows
  1 Afghan
  3 Easter baskets (empty)
  Chocolate rabbit (Hollow)
  1 carton with dyed Easter eggs
     (We used plaster eggs)
  1 bag of Easter basket grass
  1 bag of chocolate eggs in foil
  1 bag of malt balls
  1 bag of almonds & raw cashews
  1 bag of Marshmello chicks
  1 bag of small toys
  1 stuffed duck
  2 stuffed rabbits
  Water pistol

Under Bed
  1 empty glass
  1 Afghan (or quilt)
  Hand lotion

D of Bed
  Box of home improvement items
     (scattered around box)
  4 magazines

5 books
Easter basket fully packed

On Hope Chest
   Cigar box (empty)
   Lint brush
   Bob of Kleenex
   Glass of gin (½ full water)
   2 home improvement catalogues
   Globe
   Bottle of soap bubbles
   Plastic wall plates (H.I.I.)

U of Hope Chest
   Dress dummy
   Straight pin in bodice
   Yellow/blue uniform

Sewing Table
   Telephone
   3 blue ribbons (for baskets)
   Sewing machine
   Fabric, thread, bias tape, etc.
   Pair of scissors

Bench
   2 scraps of fabric

Tall Bureau U.C.
   Violin & bow (loosen) in case
   Tote bag

Low Bureau U.R.C.
   Hand mirror & brush
   Ashtray
   Kleenex dispenser w/Kleenex
   Jewelry box w/cuff links & studs

Roll of scotch tape
Hair ribbon

Bedside Table U.R.
  Ashtray
  Alarm clock
  Book matches

In Bathroom
  Turquoise plastic drinking cup
  Washcloth
  Bowl of water

In Closet
  1 three piece pin stripe suit
  1 hanger of ties
  1 suit with
    Loose change, sticks of gum,
    car keys
  1 brown suit on hanger

Doors closed upstairs

Pair of slippers under sewing table for Marshael.

ONSTAGE — 1st LEVEL

Table U of Settee
  2 Orange Crush bottles
  2 R.C. Cola bottles
  1 set car keys
  Plant (dressing)

Card Table
  Memorial book w/pen
  Brass tray w/sympathy cards
  1 folding chair (pushed in)

Desk
   Telephone
   Ashtray

Below Settee
   Standing ashtray

ONSTAGE — PARLOR

Coffee Table
   Pink carnation flower arrangement
   Glass dish w/3 boxes of matches
   Glass cig. holder w/cigarettes
   Pair of scissors (welded together)

SL of Sofa
   4 folding chairs
   Wastebasket
   "Brother" flower arrangement

U at Bookcase
   Flower arrangement on toy chest
   TV set

OUTSIDE on BALCONY
   Birds nest with 4 brown eggs

OFF STAGE L.
   Small suitcase (Pixrose)
   Collard's straw bag with:
      Pink bag w/white baby booties
      Sunglasses in case
      Small make-up bag
      Small gift wrapped for a child

Pack of opened cigarettes

In Coffin
Safety piece of ham in case Brocker can't find one that
Body
drops from sandwich.

U.C. UNDER PLATFORM — OFF STAGE
Carton of Camel Lights in brown bag
   w/book matches (Collard)
Honeysuckle (Pixrose)
2 flower baskets (Leon)
2 designer boxes of Kleenex (Katty)
1 small basket of flowers (Collard)
2 red kitchen chairs (Collard)
1 ½ full bottle of gin (Collard)
Tray with:
   2 plates w/ham and peas
   2 glasses
   2 sets of silverware
   1 container w/mustard
   2 napkins
   1 plate — 3 pieces of bread
   1 plate of ham
         (Katty brings on)
1 plate w/ham, napkin, fork, knife (Leon for Marshael)
1 plate w/10 peas, napkins, for, knife, 2 bite size pcs.
   of ham (Leon)
1 breakway plate w/ham (Pixrose)
1 platter of Rice Krispie bars (Only 2 eaten per show)
   (Leon)
1 blueberry pie (Celastex crust and filling made with
   gelatin & food coloring) (Pixrose)
½ toast (Wayne)
Napkin (Gets blood on it) (Wayne)

ACT II (Same place as above)

4 white boxes w/black veils (Leon)
2 black armbands (Leon)
1 purple violet nosegay in plastic container (Leon)
1 plate w/fried chicken drumstick (Leon)

R.

1 empty pint bottle of "Old Grandad" whiskey (Brocker)
1 full bottle of gin (Collard)
1 bottle of gin almost full (Collard)
Short ladder (Brocker)
Bunch of wild flowers (Brocker)

PERSONAL PROPS

Wooden spoons (Brocker)
Deck of porno playing cards (Brocker)
Tack (Leon)
Comb (Leon)
Pocket knife (Pixrose)
7 jelly beans (Marshael)
2 blood capsules (Wayne)

OFFSTAGE — 2nd LEVEL

2 silver cuff links in case (Katty)
1 wind-up clock (Katty)
2 hair ribbons (Katty)

SHIFT PROPS

L.

1 coffin with piece of ham by corpse head
1 coffin lid (put on in intermission)
5 jelly beans (to throw on floor by wastebasket)
Instamatic camera
Film cartridge box (for instructions)
Flip flash

Polar bear 3 piece puzzle (wood)
1 glass ¼ empty (gin)
2 glasses ½ full (gin)

UPSTAIRS

2 single sheets of newspaper (for cut out bunnies)
Shoe box with rags, neutral shoe polish
Newspaper (to put shoes on)
Basket of 3 eggs that have been blown and water added
    then re-sealed. (Do this daily or the water becomes
    polluted and the smell is grotesque)

FURNITURE LIST

BEDROOM
¾ bed
Hope chest
2 matching bureaus
   (1 tall, 1 low w/mirror)
Night stand (low table type w/drawers)
Bench
Sewing table
Dress form (dummy)

BATHROOM
Sink
Medicine cabinet

HALLWAY Down Stairs
Mission settee
End table
Standing lamp
Standing ashtray (small)
Waste basket
Combination coffee table-magazine rack
Card table
Folding chair
2 red kitchen chairs (brought on)
Narrow roll-top desk

PARLOR
Small 5' Castro sofa
Coffee table
4 wooden folding chairs (set up during action)

Coffin (brought on in 1st scene shift. It is on a rolling
  pallet)
TV set
Toy chest (with floral arrangement on it)
Built in bookcase

OUTSIDE
  Stump

PROP SHIFTS
I-1 to I-2
  Coffin WITHOUT lid moves to position (Both Men)
  Scatter 5 jelly beans DSC around waste basket (Man #1)
  THEN strike 2 folding chairs
Strike Pixrose suitcose (Man #)

INTERMISSION

DOWNSTAIRS:
  Clean up blueberry pie, jelly beans, peas
  STRIKE: (from cardtable)
    Memorial book & pen
    Brass tray w/sympathy cards
    2 gin glasses
    Small flower basket
    Gin bottle
    Kleenex box
2 folding chairs (from parlor)

SET: (on cardtable)
  1 glass (Empty)
  Wooden puzzle
  Flip flash
  Film cartridge
  Instamatic camera

Film box
Glass for Brocker (Behind Phone on desk)
Put lid on coffin

UPSTAIRS:

STRIKE
Egg carton
All bags of grass (it will be empty)
Box of home improvement items
Cowboy boots

SET
Collard's make-up bag (Dresser)
Newspaper with 3 pr. of children's shoes
Shoe box with shoe polishing items
Open can of neutral polish
Rags
Move dress dummy to C — Bedroom
Move bench to Onstage side of sewing table
Reset violin & bow on bed
Move telephone to Hope Chest
Move Easter basket with blown eggs to bedside table
2 single sheets of newspaper — end of bed

II-2 to II-3
Put coffin lid on
Put 2 flower baskets on lid (Man #1)
Strike coffin

STRIKE
Everything left on card table
Wooden puzzle
2 glasses
gin bottle
1 plate & napkin
1 flip flash box
1 film box
1 deck of cards

COSTUME PLOT

MARSHAEL
Black dress
Black bra & underwear
Black slip
Timex watchc w/black band
2 tortoise shell barettes
Pantyhose
Black shose w/bow
Grey cardigan
2 pc. black suit
White cotton shirt

LEON
2 pc. black suit
White cotton shirt
Red print tie
Black leather belt
Blue bandana handkerchief
Pen knife & comb
Watch w/brown leather band
Black ankle high shoes
Black socks
Black arm band & suit jacket

KATTY — Costume # 1
Gold watch
Wedding & engagement rings
Diamond rings
Wig
Black slip
2 pc. purple paisley dress
Matching shoes

Monogrammed handkerchief
Earrings
Add — Apron
Intermission

Costume # 2 — (Act II-Scene 1)
  2pc. pink nylon peignoir
  High heeled satin slippers
  bra

Costume # 3 — plenty of time to change
  2 pc. navy suit w/white piping
  White blouse w/soft tie
  Blue straw hat
  Cream colored slip
  Pantyhose
  Spectator shoes
  Monogramed handkerchief
  Gloves
  Handbag
  Jewelry
  Add: Blackveil

WAYNE
Costume #1 — (enters w/o jacket, cufflinks, in shirtsleeves)
  3 pc. grey pin-striped suit
  White shirt w/monogram
  Tie
  Black wing tipped shoes
  Monogramed handkerchief
  Belt w/monogram
  Digital watch
  Black socks
  Monogramed cuff links - silver
  Class ring
  I.D. bracelet

Wedding ring
Intermission
Act II — Scene 1 — disheveled version of above
(Plenty of time to change)
Costume #2 (Act II — Scene 3)
   3 pc. navy blue suit
   White shirt w/monogram (same as above)
   Same shoes
   Same jewelry & handkerchief
   Same belt
   Tie
   Add: Black arm band

COLLARD
Act I — Scene 1
Costume #1
   Red velvet dress
Bra
   Cowboy boots
   Straw hat
   Gardenia in hair

Act I — Scene 2 — Fast change in bathroom — Up right
   (has 1 page of dialogue to change)
Costume # 2
   Red plaid shirt
   Jeans
   Lavender socks
   White sneakers

Act II — Scene 2 — Remove jeans, socks & shoes fast
   Fast change — Bathroom (1 page to change)
Costume # 3 — Scene 3
   Lavender blouse
   Lavender purple wool skirt
   Brown blazer

Straw hat (wine cloored)
Sandals
Add: black veil

PIXROSE
Costume #1 — Act I - Scene 1
   Brown leather shoes
   Rose wool jumper
   White cotton blouse
   Yellow handkerchief
   Garnet broach
   Red tights
   Intermission

Costume — Act II - Scene 1
   Creme colored tights
   Long white flannel nightgown

Change during Scene 2
Costume #3 — Act II - Scene 3
   Blue & pink cotton dress
   Off white tights
   Off white long gloves
   Off white Mary Jane shoes
   Straw hat
   Add: black veil

BROCKER
   2 pc. brown suit (do not press)
   White cotton shirt
   Striped suspenders
   Brown striped tie
   White cotton socks
   Brown leather workboots
   Felt hat
   Tattoo of ship on chest
   Shirt w/egg stain on it.
   handkerchief

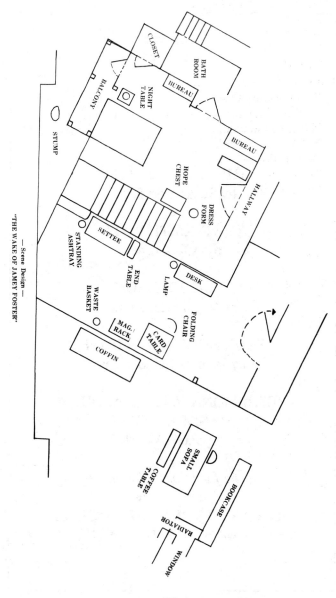

— Scene Design —
"THE WAKE OF JAMEY FOSTER"